SAINTS IN THE WORLD

SAINTS IN THE WORLD

THE ADVENTURE OF CHRISTIAN LIFE

REV. JESUS URTEAGA

 Scepter

Original title in Spanish: *El valor divino de lo humano*
(Ediciones Rialp, S.A., Madrid: 1948)
First English translation, 1959, as *Man the Saint*

Second edition, 1963
Nihil Obstat: Jacobus Mitchell
Imprimatur: Michael, *Episcopus Galviensis*
Galway, October 2, 1963

Spanish text © 1996, Ediciones Rialp, S.A., Madrid
English translation © 1997, Scepter Publishers, New York

THIRD EDITION
Published in 2009 by Scepter Publishers
P.O. Box 211, New York, N.Y. 10018
scepterpublishers.org

ISBN 978-1-59417-084-3

Printed in the United States of America

I still remember vividly, Father, the first time I heard you speak. From that moment your words became engraved on my heart as if by fire. Those words and everything I heard you say on so many unforgettable occasions since then have brought about a total transformation in my life. They impelled me to seek and to follow God, and they created that interior framework on which my whole life has taken shape.

Your words have given life not only to my soul but also to my mind. I have hung upon them; I have noted them down within minutes of hearing them; and later, in the active silence of my prayer, I have meditated upon them. I have repeated them a hundred times in my apostolate as a priest. They have become part of me.

I have written this book with the desire of reproducing your doctrine as faithfully as possible, and it is only natural that I should have used words of yours. And now I do not even know which are my own and which yours. Fortunately, there is a way of sorting them out. Perhaps in these lines there are some which you do not recognize as your own or which you would even disown: these are mine.

J. U.

Contents

Anyone familiar with this book in one of its two previous English editions (1959 and 1963) will notice that a few changes have been made, including the wording of the title. The original title, *El valor divino de lo humano* (literally, "The Divine Value of the Human"), was previously given in English as *Man the Saint.* The purpose of all our adjustments is to restore the original directness, relevance, and impact of this little book. When it first came out (in Madrid, in 1948), it had a freshness, an immediacy, a tone of voice that startled readers into action. They felt that here was a man who knew them personally, who knew exactly where they were coming from and where they needed to be going.

But that was in Spain, and that was nearly fifty years ago. To present this treasure, with no loss of impact, to American readers standing on the threshold of a new millennium, a few adaptations were in order—actually, surprisingly few. Occasionally a quotation was given with little or no source information; in such cases we have substituted another quotation, usually from the same person. Also, where these were not given, we have supplied references for biblical texts.

Originally addressed explicitly to young men, this book has a great deal to say to Christians of any age and of either gender; so the language has been made inclusive. Interestingly, though, relatively few statements or examples needed substantial adjustment. The focus is still primarily on what would traditionally be called "masculine" traits, but now and here, where we are well aware that every person has both a masculine and a feminine side, and where we do not assume that strength and courage are virtues for men only, this book needed little adjustment in order to come across as amazingly contemporary.

It is our hope that Father Urteaga's white-hot love for our Lord will succeed once more in igniting in thousands and thousands of souls that same fiery love.

When Nathanael heard Philip's exciting message "We have found him of whom Moses in the law and also the prophets wrote," he presented himself before the Lord and received from Jesus' lips one of the most profound compliments that we read in the Gospel: "Behold, an Israelite indeed, in whom is no guile!" (Jn 1: 45, 47). The Savior's loving glance was attracted, pleased, by the uprightness, the sincerity, the nobility of that man who had approached him. He saw that those human virtues were good ground, a magnificent channel through which the supernatural waters of grace could easily flow.

This is the message of Father Jesus Urteaga's *El valor divino de lo humano*, a book which has been translated into many languages. It is, indeed, an old message, traditional in God's Church. It is rooted, as we have seen, in the gospel itself, and it has come down, especially through the fathers and doctors of the Church, fresh and vigorous to our own day.

Nevertheless, it is necessary, today more than ever before, to proclaim it clearly—to make known the harmony which should exist between nature and grace, between the natural order and the supernatural, in the life of every Christian. It is, unfortunately, common among Christians to cultivate a kind of spiritual passivity in their interior life. This is the fruit of a basically negative outlook on the ascetic struggle, an outlook founded, at least unconsciously, on the false presumption that human nature is entirely corrupt and that therefore the human faculties must be annihilated and everything left to the work of grace. Thus the profoundly active dimension of the Christian life as depicted in the gospel—in the parable of the talents, the story of the barren fig tree, and so forth—is forgotten, as is this clear directive from St. Paul: "Do you not know that in a race all the runners compete, but only one receives the prize? So run that you may obtain it" (1 Cor 9: 24).

But even more dangerous is that false ascetic activism which despises the supernatural influence of grace and exalts, as being better suited to the mentality of modern times, the value of the purely natural virtues to such an extent that it degenerates into a kind of naturalistic voluntarism. In this case, again, Jesus' words are forgotten. "Apart from me," he said, "you can do nothing" (Jn 15: 5). To any and all proponents of a naturalistic, anthropocentric humanism, Father Urteaga replies bluntly: "In practice, . . . anyone who tries to do without grace and attain that ideal by purely natural means, by their own natural strength, will become no more and no less than an animal." [1]

The true Christian must avoid these two extremes, which are equally unfaithful to Christ's message and, consequently, sterile. They both ignore in practice that harmony which should exist between nature and grace. What Christ demands of us is this: "Love one another as I have loved you" (Jn 15: 12).

* *

Father Urteaga, basing his ideas on the firmest principles of ascetic theology, shows us the purpose and place of the human virtues in the edifice of sanctity.

The human virtues of which he speaks are simply those which in theological literature have traditionally been called "acquired" or "natural" virtues. It is because they can be exercised by human beings in the absence of grace that they can also be called "human" virtues. By the same token, the "infused" virtues are sometimes designated as "Christian" virtues so that they are clearly distinguished from these "acquired" or "human" virtues. It was this distinction that Pope Pius XII had in mind when, speaking of the religious and moral principles of sports activities, he said that "the physical strain thus becomes almost an exercise of human and Christian virtues. . . ." [2]

Human virtues are all those moral habits which should be possessed by a human being as such, whether Christian or non-Christian, but which the Christian, by means of grace, raises to the supernatural order.

St. Thomas Aquinas summarized the whole foundation of the Catholic doctrine on human virtues in one well-known phrase: *Gratia perficit naturam, secundum modum naturae.*[3] Grace, that is to say, operates in us according to the disposition and the facility for action which it finds in our faculties. Therefore "he whose nature is better, he, moved by grace, effects that which is perfect with greater perfection." [4] In the words of Pope Pius, "If it is true—as unquestionably it is—that supernatural grace perfects, not destroys, nature, then the edifice of evangelical perfection must be founded on the natural virtues themselves." [5]

In line with such authoritative precedents, Father Urteaga sets out to show us how necessary it is to exercise and practice the human virtues in order to arrive at the sanctity to which all Christians are called: a perfect sanctity. "You, therefore, must be perfect, as your heavenly Father is perfect" (Mt 5: 48).

It is, to be sure, a classic doctrine among theologians that the infused moral virtues, the Christian virtues, have a supernatural origin. God gives them to us by means of the sacrament of Baptism and then gives them to us again in the sacrament of Penance whenever we have the misfortune to lose them by losing sanctifying grace.

Nevertheless, these infused moral virtues do not carry within themselves any extrinsic facility for virtuous action. As Father Garrigou-Lagrange points out, facility is attained by means of the repetition of acts; it is in this way that the acquired moral virtues, the human virtues, come into being.[6] And as Father Stanislas Gillet observes, the evolution or the extinction of the Christian virtues, not at the beginning but as they develop, depends on the increase or decrease of the human virtues—which, in turn, are supernaturalized by the Christian virtues.[7]

Certainly it is true that the human virtues are not sufficient if we Christians are to aspire, as we must, to the supernatural means which will lead us to eternal life. There is no way we can love God efficaciously without the grace which cures us of sin: sanctifying grace.[8] What saves us, what makes us sons and daughters of God, is not the human virtues; it is grace, obtained by the infinite merits of Jesus Christ and poured into our hearts. In the supernatural economy as it exists, any Christian who is not in the state of grace is in mortal sin. There is no middle course. Father Urteaga states this clearly, and not without a certain irony. "However mature you may be in terms of human virtues," he says, "never for one moment forget that if you die in mortal sin you will go to hell—with all your human virtues." [9]

But this is precisely where we see most clearly that harmony between nature and grace in which, we repeat, the sanctity of Christians consists. Within the Christian, the supernatural flow of grace permeates the whole natural organism of human virtues, making all the acts of those virtues divinely efficacious, valuable, meritorious, in the eyes of God. Thus even the most mundane things can acquire a divine value.

One cannot violate this unity, this harmony, without

establishing a deep cleft in the Christian life; for on the plane of action, natural strength and supernatural virtues go together and are mutually interwoven. The supernatural virtues give supernatural efficacy; the human virtues create a proper disposition and facility.

Again we may make use of the teaching of Pope Pius XII to sum up the theology of the human virtues: "As you well know, the possession and formation of the so-called natural virtues disposes toward a supernatural dignity of life, especially when a person practices and cultivates them in order to be a good Christian, and a fit herald of Christ." [10]

* *

To come across a book on the importance of the human virtues is particularly interesting in these days when, through the inspiration of the Holy Spirit, Christians are realizing more and more forcefully the possibility and the necessity of sanctifying themselves in the midst of the world by bringing Christ into all fields of human activity.

Our model, as always, is Jesus: *perfectus Deus, perfectus homo.*[11] "Though he was . . . God" (Phil 2:6), he wished nevertheless, through an infinite love for the human race, to come down to earth and live among us. "And the Word became flesh and dwelt among us" (Jn 1:14). Christ took on himself everything human, with the one exception of sin (see Heb 2:17 and 4:15). In conformity with the example and the commandment of our Lord, we Christians have to go out into this world in which we live, and by our presence—a presence vibrating with love—bring to the very heart of the world, to every nook and cranny of it, the redeeming blood of the Savior. This call to participate in the work of our Redeemer requires that we stay closely united to him and faithfully follow his example. We must, like our Lord, take upon ourselves—incorporate, make part of our own flesh—all human things, with that one exception of sin. We must be like our God, who "so loved the world" that he spared no expense "that the world might be saved" (Jn 3: 16–17).

Everything that is genuinely *human*, and properly ordered toward its true end, can have a *divine* value if it is offered to the Lord with rectitude of intention. Professional work and healthy relaxation, social and political activities, scientific discoveries and philosophic investigations, together with all the little details of ordinary daily life—all these things can and must be incorporated into God's plan. Thus will the followers of Christ make his reign over all human activity an obvious reality.

Furthermore, the function of giving example, an apostolate which belongs to every Christian living in the midst of humanity—"You are the light of the world" (Mt 5: 14)—demands that the supernatural virtues should be embodied, or incarnated; that is, founded on the human virtues. Emmanuel Cardinal Suhard, speaking with reference to priests, expresses this truth very forcefully:

> If [a priest] wants the faithful to imitate him, he must, in an age made skeptical by the abuse of propaganda, first of all influence others by his own example and by his supernatural virtues. People today are always taking notes and making comparisons. If the priest's supernatural virtues are not supported by genuine, supernaturalized *natural virtues*, they will seem odd or despicable. Being made a priest does not dispense one from being loyal, or courageous, or magnanimous, or from having a keen sense of justice. Without these qualities the priest will not appeal to what is best in modern man and humanism, and he should not be surprised that he does not.[12]

Preface

Notwithstanding the sound theological doctrine with which it is permeated, *Saints in the World* (entitled *Man the Saint* in the two previous English editions) is not a theological book. Father Urteaga, who holds doctorates in both theology and law, has not written it for an elite group of theologians or moralists. No, this is a book written from the heart, born of direct contact with ordinary men and women. Perhaps its most salient and constant characteristic is a passionate love for the person of Jesus of Nazareth, the "carpenter's son" who was, although divine, completely human, as well. A deep sadness, caused by the indifference and mediocrity of so many Christians, cannot suppress the supernatural joy in these pages written face to face with the Lord. The author writes with a youthful pen, vibrating, sharp; his words go straight to the heart, bringing warmth and light, inspiring in his readers that healthy restlessness which finds peace only in a more exacting fidelity to Christ's message.

INTRODUCTION

MY PEOPLE HAVE COMMITTED TWO EVILS: THEY HAVE FORSAKEN ME, THE FOUNTAIN OF LIVING WATERS, AND HEWED OUT CISTERNS FOR THEMSELVES, BROKEN CISTERNS THAT CAN HOLD NO WATER.

— Jeremiah 2: 13

RUNNING AWAY FROM GOD

Open your eyes for a moment, and you will see your God in tears. Open your eyes, and you will see the utter confusion of this age in which we live. In all the history of humanity has there ever been worse chaos? Men and women, young and old, rich and poor, have all run away from their God. They have unshouldered the sweet yoke of the Almighty and have thrown it far away. The nations of the earth have rebelled against their Lord and against his Christ. Perhaps with the prophet (see Jer 5: 4) we think that it is only the uncultured and the illiterate who are ignorant of the ways and precepts of Yahweh. We turn to the ones with influence, the ones with power, and we speak to them of God. Surely they, at least, will know his commandments. "But they all alike had broken the yoke, they had burst the bonds" (Jer 5: 5).

Look at them—they are all running madly from their God. And then, in their wild, irrational flight, they suddenly stumble against the cross standing dark and lonely in their path. They keep on running to escape from this cross, leaving it behind, alone and forgotten. A great army of determined creatures united in their hatred of their Creator. And the mad torrent of those who hate him sweeps along with it the indifferent and the lukewarm.

Where are they going? They have left God far behind, and now they go in search of something worth believing in, something to quench their thirst. Now it is the turn of unbelievers, nailed to the cross of their own unbearable lives, to cry "I thirst"—and they do not know where to look for water. For them the earth is a hateful place, and heaven is so far off. But where are they going? They seek new gods and new creeds. They all, whether it be in their nation or race, or money or whatever, seek something which none of these things can give. They try to replace worship of God, who is our Father, with worship of his footsteps in the filthy mire of their evil ways.

The ancient cry of the Holy Spirit is woeful and still new: "My people have committed two evils: they have forsaken me, the fountain of living waters, and hewed out cisterns for themselves, broken cisterns, that can hold no water." And nowadays it is these cistern makers who shape the destinies of the nations of the earth. They know only hate, nothing of love. The education and formation of the people of tomorrow is in their dirty hands, crooked and deformed from fondling their money It is these who talk of peace, who try to console the victims of war, the sick, the mutilated. These are the leaders in the present disorder; and they vainly promise order and prosperity. They speak of one great family that will unite the rich with the poor, executives with employees, children with their parents, soldiers with politicians. They speak of this great union which will ignore Christ and laugh at his Church. These vain cistern makers, in their mad escape from God, tell us of new "sacraments" which can give life to rotting skeletons!

ABOUT THIS GOD AND THIS WORLD

We are not going to concern ourselves with the complicated causes of this present atheism. That is a scientific question best left to the scholars. What I want to speak about is that enormous task, human but at the same time supernatural, which every Christian who lives at the dawning of this new millennium must undertake. The threat of utter ruin hovers over the world. The problem is urgent. We must act *now*, immediately.

First of all, I want you to open your eyes wide and examine that lukewarm, worthless life which you are now leading. Naturally I am interested in the lives of those creatures who have fled from God, but your life interests me far more. Never forget that that life of yours which you have been leading for so many years, so important to you and to me, is one of the real causes of this disease which is ravaging the world. You too are guilty!

The problems of this time, the dawning of the new millennium, are various and urgent—much too urgent for you to sit quietly and enjoy yourself, letting others look for solutions. Surely you attach some importance to the lives of those around you. Now don't even try to tell me that one life like yours can't make a real difference, that one person can't do much of anything. The sons and daughters of God must surely be at least as influential as the children of the devil. In the whole of Christendom there must surely be young people strong and healthy enough to put a stop to the vicious onslaughts of their enemies.

Have you too forgotten God? Do you realize that right now you are living and working side by side with saints?

Whatever you may think of yourself as an individual, you must realize that you carry within you the possibility, the seed, of a marvelous human life on which supernatural life—a life of grace—can be firmly based, and that this will make of you, not simply one more person, but a real daughter or son of God with all the strength and courage of our prophets.

Who says disregard for human virtues is humility? Today more than ever before, every Christian must be first of all a truly human being. This world is in urgent need of Christians who are strong and courageous individuals, loyal soldiers, hard workers. It needs people who have learned to unite a life of prayer with a life of daily work; who have learned to incorporate into their intimate union with God a happy social life with their parents and other relatives, with their friends, and even their enemies. Are we not ashamed to face the world as men and women when we live our religion like cowards, in a way that is insipid, timid, and altogether ridiculous?

Do not for one moment think that because Christianity puts into practice the supernatural virtues, it is no longer compatible with ordinary life. Christianity *is*, above all, *life*: supernatural life united with natural life. Some people (often, though not necessarily, the more intelligent) manage to understand the supernatural life; but the true value, the intrinsic value, of our natural, human life remains unknown or forgotten by very many. Our human nature will always have to be the basis and foundation of any serious, deep, and healthy interior life.

In this little book, then, we will say something about human formation. We will see that the saints were people who lived the human virtues of truthfulness, uprightness, courage, while at the same time developing their own individual personalities. We will speak about the hard and monotonous work of our everyday lives in the midst of a busy world. We will speak of the courage which animates people in love; we will speak of divine "foolishness," of generosity, of sorrow, of death, of joy. We will see that for a true Christian, life is a great adventure.

Several books have been written on the God who became man. I want, now, to speak to you about that same God, but more especially about the man, about the earth on which he lived, about the struggle of life. I want to explain to you how we can, and how we must, live with that same God in our work and in our play by way of the books that we read and the tools that we use, in the city and in the country... We will speak of that age of fire which is approaching rapidly—an age not of triumph but of war. We will consider together the position of the Christian in relation to other people: how saints live and work as the Church wants them to live and work. Together we will have a look at some of the problems of Christianity in the world today.

In short, I want to talk to you about human virtues. I myself have invented nothing of what I am going to say. I myself simply fell in love with those virtues which are natural, but which are at the same time the only basis of the supernatural virtues, when I saw them practiced in the lives of a few of the individuals who introduced me to my God.

The concept of holiness which I have to offer you is not in any way new. What I want to do is to help you see and understand the enormous importance of the human factor in the Christian and in the saint. So we will speak, not of what the Christian must do in order to become a saint, but rather of that which all human beings have within themselves and must sanctify.

Never forgetting God, who is with us on every page, and always recognizing the primary importance of grace, without which all human efforts are useless, we will not concern ourselves here directly with the supernatural virtues which every Christian must try to acquire. We are going to speak about the creature of flesh and blood, the human being as such, and then consider especially the human being who wants to become a saint—looking at saintliness not as an end in itself, but as something leading us to our God.

On all these questions there is a lot that could be said, and many different ways of saying it. The important thing for a writer to do is to choose a truly Christian method of dealing with them: a method that is spiritually and intellectually correct and at the same time operative, so that the reader is engaged, impelled to action, and set on fire with an active zeal. It is this dynamic fire which I am especially trying to enkindle in your heart.

These pages have been written in spasmodic outbursts, without any attempt at style or rhetoric, without any external or formal unity. They have been written with a violent pen animated by a heart on fire. Read through them quickly—they have been written quickly. How could you expect me to talk to you slowly and calmly? There's no time. So much to be done, and we're the ones who have to do it—you and I!

To the Restless and the Rebellious

Are you going to keep on thinking that for us Christians, life is a useless, passive passage of time? No, life is a thrilling game in which the winners are always the lovers, the hard workers, the ambitious. Everything has its own particular use. The disappointments, the obstacles, the difficulties—all those things which are considered to be of no value in life—can be converted into genuine gems of great worth, if only we are ready to act.

There are so many Christians who drift along in the same monotonous current of life as the other tired mortals, unthinking, happy to be one of the crowd. Are you one of those? Are you content to follow the tired and monotonous rhythm of the others, the slow step of the insipid, of the mediocre, of those who never aim at anything higher than what their own downcast eyes can see? If you are, then I tell you straight out: close this book right now. It will only disappoint you. It has nothing to contribute to a base and useless way of life. These pages have been written in a vivid awareness of the presence of God. They are not for the apathetic.

I am writing them for the restless and the rebellious, for those who are dissatisfied with their own lives and the lives of others. For those capable of violent passions—because it is they who will wrench from the children of Satan their ill-gotten glory. For those who realize that to gain Life we must surrender our lives. For all those with high and noble ideals.

As St. Josemaría Escrivà pointed out, all of our "world crises are crises of saints." [1] They all have a solution; they've got to. And we will find that solution—in Christianity, in the Gospels. Stop being pessimistic. Amid the ruins and debris of our pitiable humanity there are still women and men who hold the secret of that solution. And don't say there are hardly any left. There are enough to found a new race, a noble race, of human beings. These are people whose hearts are saturated with God: courageous men and women; passionate followers of Christ; "crazy" people bursting with faith, bursting with hope, bursting with love. They alone have the secret which others vainly seek.

Wait a little while and you will see, here and there, some of these saints of our own time coming forward and putting Christ at the pinnacle of every human activity—in all places, at all times. There is no legitimate way of life, or kind of work, that is beneath the dignity of a good Christian. There is no occupation, unless it's something immoral in itself, in which a Christian cannot and should not take a leading part.

So, that is what we have to do, you and I: make Christ the topmost point of all human actions. But if we want to do that, we must first understand what it is that we humans have which is worth sanctifying, and how we are meant to sanctify it. The coward who has not the courage to live like a human being can never be a saint. Saints never do anything by halves. Every saint is the bearer of a divine message, and God demands everything, without reserve.

We must remember that the God who can no longer be seen is still the very same as that God who, burning with love for you and for me, became a little child in order to play with other little children, and later took the form of a host to be the food of sickly people.

The Lord continues to do wild things in our own day. I am going to tell you something about them in the pages which follow. If we happen to meet someday in the midst of this busy world, ask me about the latest crazy deeds of this God who loves us. Then I will tell you everything he did, and you will love him with me. The crazy things he did for you may inspire you to seek and find a true and worthy outlet for your loyal rebellion, for your anxious restlessness, for your legitimate unhappiness, for that holy dissatisfaction which you share with other sons and daughters of God.

1. SAINTS, PAGANS, COWARDS, PIETISTS

TO BE A SAINT IN THIS WORLD IS TO DEVELOP TO THE FULL
ONE'S HUMAN NATURE.

  — Arnold Rademacher, *Religion and Life*

SCOFFING

The attitude of those who fled from God centuries ago has degenerated into a cold and bitter paganism. There are very few heretics left in the modern world. Those who abandon the one true God very soon fall victim to the most barren dryness of soul. They are simply pagans; and today they can be seen all around us, straining their sightless eyes, vainly seeking that happiness for which their instincts cry out; groping about in the dark, blindly trying to find the way, the truth, and the life. We try to help them. We have told them a thousand times to look to our Christ. They have tried to look, but they see nothing. We shout at them that Christ is alive, really alive—the same man that he always was and always will be—but the force of our arguments is dissipated by their cold indifference. And yet it is easy enough to understand the spiritual bankruptcy and the bitterness of these poor pagans when we read the cynical challenge in their eyes: "Show us by your *lives* that Christ is alive." Their argument is all too on-target. We cannot expect them to be won over by treatises on apologetics and theology, so many of which are dreadfully dry and formal. Their challenge is fair enough: "Show us by your *lives* that Christ is alive."

We look around us, among our Christian contemporaries, for lives to which we could point as examples and models for those who have lost their faith; and we are torn with grief when we cannot find them. It is a cause of bitter regret to see the insipid and crumbling spectacle we present to the world after twenty centuries of so-called progress. Our world is full of living Christians, and yet it is the lifeless who are in command. We have plenty of churches, but so few good lives. All we lack is lives—lives to inspire the dead; to convince the skeptical; to strengthen the wills of poor, weak mortals; to enlighten the minds of the diseased; to soften the selfish hearts of greedy materialists. Passionate lives; generous lives; lives ablaze with love. So few good lives!

Saddened by the mediocrity of the Christian world, ashamed of seeking in vain for living beacons to enlighten the pagan darkness, disheartened by the futility of our efforts, we seek in our Christian past what we cannot find in the present. And we show the pagans the glorious lives of our saints.

"What do you mean by a saint?" they ask with a sarcastic smile. We raise our thoughts to heaven and try to overcome our rage. We bite our tongues and force ourselves to smile. These pagans have the audacity to sneer at our saints. For these perverted souls a saint is no more than a ghostly statue carved in a stiff, uncomfortable pose, hidden away in a corner of some church, and surrounded by the sick and the elderly.

These pagans say: "What are saints? They're simply poor fools who set out, full of enthusiasm, to put into practice that silly motto 'pray and work,' and then always stopped halfway doing nothing useful—just praying all the time, thumping their breasts, saying rosaries, neglecting the ordinary work that people are supposed to do.

"What are saints? Pale, sickly wretches for whom life held only disdain and contempt, and who ran away from it all to meditate on death. Their own health lost, they used up what little strength they had in despising the strong. Dark figures, wrapped in their religious habits, who never saw the light of day; ghastly figures stalking about the deserted mountainsides like the giants of old, frightening their peaceful neighbors."

That is how pagans think of saints. And they smile sardonically when we mention them.

But our saints are not ghosts or statues. They are people, real people, of all ages and descriptions. Some of them are old and move slowly; others are young and run lightly with the spirit of youth. Some do wear religious habits; others, regular clothes. Some go bareheaded; some are in tattered dress, others in business suits. Soldiers on foot or on horseback; pilgrims covered in dust; saints in royal velvet, and saints in the chains of slaves! All ordinary, but inspiring, human beings.

And still the pagans hate them and sneer at them. At best, saints provide them with one more subject for poetry and daydreaming. They may admire their zeal, their sensitivity, their love of nature . . . But, for their God, these modern pagans have only contempt.

And for the faithful themselves—for those affiliated by baptism to the true doctrine of Christ—what is a saint? Again we are ashamed of the stupid things we see and hear. For many of the faithful, the saints are objects of pity: poor creatures, in centuries gone by who spent all their lives on their knees. Eccentrics who by outlandish penances and austerity became God's pets. And the idea that God spoils his saints and pampers them still persists in the minds of our faithful. They run to the saint to ask favors, they passionately kiss her plaster image, they gaze spellbound at his face of molded clay, they leave a few coins as a token of their love. They pray for a faithful husband, a good wife, the recovery of something lost. And there are special days on which they think it is easier to get these things.

That is what the saints mean nowadays. Poor saints! Christ's holy Church singled them out as examples for us, and now they are nothing more than ugly figures of cheap clay glued to wooden pedestals painted to look like marble. Not all of us have this idea, but, unfortunately, many people do. We can hardly complain, then, at what atheists think when they see us, who are supposed to be Christians, so far off track. To confuse our saints with plaster figures is absurd!

"LIVES OF THE SAINTS"

Again they ask us: "What do you mean by 'a saint'?" So, we reluctantly take out one of those books called "lives of the saints"—traditionally a book in black covers, a deep, forbidding black, a book often printed in large type so that it can be read easily by the bifocal set. In these books we read of unpleasant characters with very little vitality and no sense of humor, who at the tender age of four or five showed a strong aversion to the base and perverted world around them. Sometimes these examples on which we are asked to model our lives are supposed to have been children who never behaved as children—who never played childish tricks, never laughed, never cried. When we were children we asked Santa Claus to bring us a teddy bear or a doll, a train set, a drum, and so forth. But the saints, according to these books, were always above such silly, childish desires.

When these books deal with a teenager or young adult, they set out to exalt his modesty, but what they actually describe is utter timidity. They speak of purity in such a way that it appears to be sheer cowardice. And they very often confuse sanctity with wisdom. If they are forced to speak of a saint who happened to be no genius, they carefully hide the fact and instead point out the habits of mental prayer which she always kept secret—a fact which they mention with regret.

Why are they afraid to tell us that externally the saints had all the characteristics of ordinary people? They seem to think that sanctity involves bearing on one's forehead a mark distinguishing one from other mortals, as if sanctity were simply one profession among others.

(We are speaking now only of what we read. It is better not to discuss in any detail those unsightly plaster statues which we see so often—with their hideous faces, exaggerated poses, unnatural expressions.)

This is a third mistaken idea that people have of saints, and those pious authors are the cause of it, because all they show us is, in one instance after another, a shower of divine grace on an insipid and sickly nature. I have often thought of writing a book with the title *The Defects of the Saints*;[1] but it would be very difficult to find any human weaknesses in the lifeless creatures described in these books. The authors always try to hide them. And what a shame that is. How encouraging it would be for us to see the natural defects of the saints and the means they used to overcome them. That is why many people find "lives of the saints" boring, tiresome, and deceptive. People like you and me want a model whom we can imitate: a really *human* being, a friend to encourage us in our struggles. Real persons hope to find some real personality in the saints. But in most cases any personality we find is disfigured or completely deformed.

PIETISM

ACCORDING AS THE SENSE OF THE OVERALL IMPORTANCE OF GOD HIMSELF IS ERASED FROM PEOPLE'S CONSCIENCES, CHRISTIANITY BECOMES MORE AND MORE DEGRADED. AND IN THE SAME PROPORTION IT LOSES ITS TRANSFORMING INFLUENCE.

— Jacques Leclercq, *Dialogue of God and Man*

These "lives of the saints" have prepared the ground for the growth of a monstrous weed, a mixture of saint in appearance and coward in fact—a kind of hybrid plant, as it were, which sprouts in the obscure shelter of our churches. For want of a better name, I shall call it the "pietist."

This kind of person has, thank God, become much rarer in recent decades. However, there are still some pietists around, and they tend to give piety a bad name. Many people shy away from a serious pursuit of sanctity because they think it entails pietistic behavior. So, to clear up any such misconception, I will spend a few moments discussing pietism and how it differs from true sanctity.

If those who have fled from God were to reconsider their position and look for the truth in the lives of those who call themselves his children, they would find it very difficult to find any grain of truth in the phenomenally unreal, prudish life of a pietist. This shallow creature wants to become a saint, true enough, but as Father R.-L. Bruckberger says, "Whilst the longings of a saint are for God, the pietist has his heart set on sanctity for its own sake." [2]

Pietists are spiritually shortsighted. They see the world as being full of evil and perverse individuals, and they retreat into their own selfish world. They complain of how the priests of God are being mistreated, but it would never occur to them to get up some courage and defend one of those priests, or to make a spirited attack on the enemies of the Church. Under a cloak of prudence they are really cowards. In moments of strong emotion they may implore God to send down fire from heaven to destroy all these wicked people—but always to destroy; this type never experiences the noble ambition of trying to save. In times of peace some foolish parents may even set them up as an example to their children, because of their apparent goodness, but in times of war they will always be despised. One of the many human virtues they lack is that of ordinary courage. They have no ambition, no global outlook. In spiritual matters they are blind.

Pietists attach extraordinary importance to external forms which they stupidly think will make them saints. They are never very original; they counterfeit the originals, but are themselves ignorant of technique and void of imagination. They try to imitate particular traits in a favorite saint, but make no effort to understand the underlying motivations of that saint's life.

Pietists, in other words, are people content to live the outward forms of an interior life of which they know nothing.

Inherent in pietism is a lack of dignity in the most intimate relations between one's soul and God. If we hold our heads up straight when we talk to one another, why should we get into all kinds of contortions when we speak to God?

If pietists were helped to get over their nonsensical vanity, in many cases their falsifying parody of holiness would die out. If no one would bother to look at them when they show the whites of their eyes, if no one would pay any attention to them when they demurely lower their heads, they would soon give up their pietism. You will easily recognize these sanctimonious individuals:

they wear several crosses and all sorts of medals, and they put holy cards in every book they read, but they have no inclination to do any hard work. When an occasion arises that calls for self-denial, for the making of some little sacrifice, they completely lack generosity.

They neglect their responsibilities, they make no new friends. You must never approach them expecting a warm reception, because their hearts are cold and hard. You must be very careful in your conversation, because they are easily shocked. You can speak to them of novenas and litanies, but not of interior life, because they won't know what you are talking about. You can talk of religious ceremonies; you can discuss which parishes have Mass at what time; but you can't discuss any kind of personal apostolate, because they do not even know the meaning of the term.

That the Church has always considered pietism an aberration is evident from the way St. John of the Cross describes the pietists of his day:

> Many can never have enough of listening to counsels and learning spiritual precepts, and of possessing and reading many books which treat of this matter, and they spend their time on all these things rather than on works of mortification and the perfecting of the inward poverty of spirit which should be theirs. Furthermore, they burden themselves with images and rosaries which are very curious; now they put down one, now take up another; now they change about, now change back again; now they want this kind of thing, now that, preferring one kind of cross to another, because it is more curious.[3]

Pietists may set themselves up as saintly model Christians, but the lives they lead will never convince anyone that Christ is still alive. Blue-collar workers who look down on their companions, white-collar workers who are short-tempered or bad-mannered, students who do not study—their behavior is far from edifying.

Pietism is simply a vice like any other vice. There is no such thing as a vocation to it. It is a monstrosity, a caricature of Christianity, and, like all other caricatures, it must be banished.

SLANDER

MIRIAM AND AARON SPOKE AGAINST MOSES. . . . "WHY, THEN, WERE YOU NOT AFRAID TO SPEAK AGAINST MY SERVANT MOSES?" AND . . . BEHOLD, MIRIAM WAS LEPROUS, AS WHITE AS SNOW. AND AARON TURNED TOWARD MIRIAM, AND BEHOLD, SHE WAS LEPROUS.

— Numbers 12: 1–10

To the challenge of all those who say that Christ is not alive, we thought of replying by showing them the lives of some contemporary Christians. We were going to present this or that particular person as a sterling example. But as we passed along the ranks of our fellow Christians, trying to pick out the best, time after time the cry escaped from our lips: "No, not that one." And we kept repeating that lamentable cry as we went along. Ashamed and embarrassed, we finally had to stop so that these nonbelievers would not see the depressing spectacle which we modern Christians present. We could not sincerely and advantageously say anything of the present, so we looked hopefully to the past, to the lives of the saints. But that, too, got us nowhere. Certainly there are some good books on this subject, but the choice we made was so unfortunate that nobody was convinced.

We have already said something of what those souls thirsting for truth would find in the darkness of our churches; but we have said nothing of what they would find flowing from the malicious tongues of the "Christian" backbiters who throng our streets. As Christians, we should truly be ashamed of ourselves. We are trying to re-Christianize society, but first of all we need to re-Christianize ourselves.

If you are a true rebel, then here are two more things for you to revolt against: jealousy and slander. These are two aspects of one hideous sin which is flourishing among followers of Christ—followers who have long forgotten not only that Christ gave us a new commandment, the commandment of love, but even that there exists among the cardinal virtues one called justice. You yourself have probably noticed that these days people speak with great "charity," but with very little justice. Unjust criticism goes over so well—it's really quite fashionable! We are certainly experts at inventing puzzles. Gossip and backbiting are no longer vices; we prefer to call them "just being honest"!

Haven't you ever been the victim of this type of "honesty"? Actually that is a mark of all good Christians, a kind of seal which God lovingly imprints on the lives of all his own. If you do not wish to do anything useful with your life, anything great, then let yourself be influenced by the silly, malicious criticism of jealous gossips. Have you never felt that exasperation—if we were not Christians, we would call it despair—of seeing people misinterpret your most innocent acts? You tell me sorrowfully that you have. You tell me your sad story which is the story of so many good people. How you put all your heart into that undertaking, with such high aims. Your ambitions were purely supernatural, your sights all set on the harvest day. You had thought it all out before taking the first step. The expense was of no concern to you, you were so enthusiastic about it all. And then what happened? What did you hear?

"They make their tongue sharp as a serpent's, and under their lips is the poison of vipers" (Ps 140:3). Tongues wagged and spit filth, casting suspicion on your divine ideals, on your noble human ambitions. The cross of slander lay upon your shoulders. And all the time you were living so close to God. But then you remembered that the delicate children are always the most spoiled by their parents, and you felt proud to be treated like a healthy kid, and you smiled.

Never be so foolish as to try to please everybody. If you try to do anything seriously and properly you are likely to feel the lash of calumny. Just always remember these words from Tertullian: "Who, on inquiry, does not join us, and joining us, does not wish to suffer, that he may purchase for himself the whole grace of God, that he may win full pardon from God by paying his own blood for it? For all sins are forgiven to a deed like this. That is why on being sentenced by you, on the instant we render you thanks. There is a rivalry between God's ways and man's; we are condemned by you, we are acquitted by God." [4]

Do your best to please God, and you can be sure that others will do their best to bring about your downfall. It is indeed a sorry situation when people feel they have to hide their own weaknesses by hurling insults at the work of others. But, unfortunately, that's the way it is. Nothing is more painful to the barren than to hear talk of children. Envy always yields the bitter fruit of calumny.

The same thing happens over and over again. When will we put a stop to it? There is always someone who asks, What do these newcomers want? What right do they have to encroach on our field of work? "These last worked only one hour, and you have made them equal to us who have borne the burden of the day and the scorching heat" (Mt 20:12).

We were all waiting with the good father for his prodigal son to return from the unhappy life he was leading. We have a great interest in the notoriously sinful and the newly healthy in Zacchaeus and Mary Magdalene; we are especially interested in the ones who fled from God. Christ did come, after all, to find the lost sheep. But there is one man in the parable of the prodigal son (Lk 15: 11–32) who bewails the return of the prodigal, and that man is his brother. "He was angry and refused to go in." He is thinking now that there will be an end to the privileges he has enjoyed as an only son. From now on he will have to share his father's attentions with his brother. He wants to preserve the status quo; he has been, after all, for all practical purposes, in complete control of his father's estate. What has this interloper come for, "this son of yours"?—he won't even call him his brother—"I never disobeyed your command; yet you never gave me a kid, that I might make merry with my friends. But when this son of yours came, who has devoured your living with harlots, you killed for him the fatted calf!" His jealousy and hatred even lead him to shout out the past sins of the converted prodigal. The father says, "It was fitting to make merry and be glad, for this your brother was dead, and is alive; he was lost, and is found." But all argument is useless. The ears of Envy do not hear the voice of Love; the envious listen only to the echoes of their own bitterness. And if they can find no faults to broadcast, they invent them; it was true in Jesus' day, and it is no less true in ours. Have you never come across this in supposedly good Christians?

Can you call this honesty? Why do we insist on misusing words? If this kind of thing qualified as honest, then all dealings with souls would be nothing but business affairs. No, the real name for this envious attitude is supernatural blindness. The apostle John has two things to say on this point: "By this we may be sure that we know him, if we keep his commandments. He who says 'I know him' but disobeys his commandments is a liar, and the truth is not in him" (1 Jn 2: 34); and "Jesus answered them, 'Do not murmur among yourselves'" (Jn 6: 43). Whenever you are indignant, whenever you are in a rage, keep a firm hold on your tongue. Remember this old Chinese proverb: "The calumny that comes out of a person's mouth is like a team of runaway horses which will be tamed only with the greatest difficulty."

Particularly impressive in this connection is a certain instruction sent by Paul to Timothy. "In the presence of God and of Christ Jesus and of the elect angels," he says, "I charge you to keep these rules without favor, doing nothing from partiality" (1 Tim 5: 21). One of "these rules" is: "Never admit any charge against an elder except on the evidence of two or three witnesses" (5: 19).

Whatever you whisper in the ear of a friend will soon be shouted in the ears of the crowd. You will try to wipe out the harm you have caused to the honor of that individual, of that institution, of that idea, and you will fail. Slander always leaves its mark.

May we never have to be ashamed of anything we have said—because the day will come when every word will be judged. The Divine Word, Truth itself, will judge the cruel words of the untruthful. And they can expect no leniency; they had their chance.

Let me tell you a story. I had the opportunity of following closely the unfaltering steps of a certain man who suffered the spiteful attacks of this kind of slander. Everything he did was criticized—his work, his way of thinking, his words, his actions. Every tongue whispered, "I've heard something about that man . . ." One "good" Christian said to another, "Guess what I heard?"

O Lord, what will become of us if every unfounded word we speak—all this evil talk, this gossip, these lies—must be burned away before we can enter the kingdom of heaven? I often wonder why someone doesn't put a stop to these injustices. If stolen goods must be restored in order for the thief to get forgiveness, it should be obvious that the same holds true with regard to a person's reputation! Do people really think that gold is of more value than a person's good name?

As I was saying a little while ago, many people who have forgotten the human virtues attend to the external forms of charity while completely neglecting justice. These people ought to be told that charity consists not in soft words or polite phrases, but in real love manifested in deeds. Remember: "'Lord, Lord,'... 'I never knew you'" (Mt 7: 21–23).

I wept when I saw the innocent life which this excellent man was living. He never complained or tried to defend himself. Tears filled his eyes when he read the letters sent by his few remaining friends—letters telling him what was being said about him, and urging him to change his ways. But no, he never uttered the slightest protest. The seed which had been hidden in the good ground, in the fertile soil, had taken firm root in God.

Those with little imagination slandered him on a small scale. The ones with the most personality made him suffer the most.

"How long will you set upon a man to shatter him, all of you, like a leaning wall, a tottering fence? They only plan to thrust him down from his eminence. They take pleasure in falsehood. They bless with their mouths, but inwardly they curse" (Ps 62: 34). But he still trusted in God—in whom else could he have trusted? "He only is my rock and my salvation, my fortress; I shall not be shaken" (Ps 62: 6).

I watched his reactions throughout this persecution. Time is often slow to vindicate the innocent, but in the end it always does. When that moment came for him, I observed his behavior. His slanderers never made a move; he was the only one that did. He added a further gem to his crown of heroism by joyfully advancing to meet them and asking them to forget the past.

Never fear the gossips who shout and who point accusing fingers, for one can always reply to such shouters with the simple truth, and silence them at once. But that is not how you will be calumniated. No; the lie will be whispered in people's ears, with confidential words of feigned pity. That is how hypocrites have always worked—those perverted hypocrites, sleek and shining on the outside but cutting as steel within. They never say it to your face; they haven't the courage.

"The Lord said to Cain, 'Why are you angry and why has your countenance fallen? If you do well, will you not be accepted?'" (Gen 4: 6–7). When you speak to anyone, never be ashamed to look him in the eye!

Think for a moment of the people who are the worst slanderers: the hard-hearted, the petty, the thwarted, the jealous . . . You have nothing to fear from such wretches. They cannot hurt you. Are you ready to meet all calumnies head-on and thus exterminate them completely?

One of these days we will have to tell certain persons who dare to call themselves Christian: "I'm tired of putting up with your slander. I'm prepared to suffer any harm you might do to my own good name, but I refuse to tolerate the insults you are offering to my holy mother the Church with your slanderous lies." If as Christians they decide to ignore the divine law of charity, as human beings they should be made to reckon with human justice. If their conscience does not accuse them of their evildoing before God, then earthly tribunals should condemn them.

So, now, go on your way. Continue your straight-ahead journey undeterred by the barking dogs you will meet in your path. Keep in mind these words of St. Josemaría Escrivà:

> Willpower. Energy. Example. What has to be done is done . . . without hesitation . . . without worrying about what others think. . . . Otherwise . . . Teresa of Ahumada [would not have been] St. Teresa; nor Iñigo of Loyola, St. Ignatius. God and daring! *Regnare Christum volumus!* We want Christ to reign! [5]

SANCTITY

What is the great defect, what is so wrong in the lives of present-day Christians, which renders the Church powerless to win over the indifferent and the atheistic? What is the great error in our lives, that we cannot be offered as examples to the pagans? What is wrong with us, that we cannot convince anyone that Christ is really alive? Why are we Christians of today considered incapable of renewing the world, when in fact we are the only ones in possession of the vital energy needed for such a transformation?

The answer is that the followers of Christ no longer have any real desire for sanctity. The children of God have become mediocre and lukewarm. What a fearful contradiction that is! Christians laugh, exactly like pagans, when you speak to them of perfection.

\ O Lord, is there any way to wake them up? How are we to convince those who bear the sacred name of Christ that they have a pressing duty to pursue sanctity? The command of Christ is absolute, admitting of no exceptions: "You, therefore, must be perfect, as your heavenly

Father is perfect" (Mt 5: 48). And the great Apostle of the Gentiles continues to cry out,"For this is the will of God: your sanctification" (1 Thess 4: 3).

Sanctity must be, then, within the reach of everyone, since God himself imposes it on all alike. He does not demand of everyone a sanctity which will manifest itself in extraordinary ways, such as prophesying or the working of miracles, but what he does ask is that every one of us should do extraordinarily well our own everyday work. Your motto should be: "Do what should be done, and do it well"—which means, among other things, with love, for the God of love. Any Christian who does not strive for that sanctity, who does not seek that perfection, shows the most profound ignorance of the real meaning of life, of religion, of faith, of God.

If we are to be of any use in this world, we must be saints! Otherwise our lives will not have sufficient strength to pull back toward God those souls who have run away from him. But we must not be disheartened by the examples which those "lives of the saints" present for our imitation. Never be discouraged—the saints were not really like that. Those books give a very distorted picture.

All our doubts will vanish and our courage will return if we simply look at the gospel. In the gospel we see that most of Christ's life was thirty years of ordinary work and ordinary obedience, a life like that of everybody else. When Jesus was a little boy he never made little birds of clay and then breathed life into them so he could see them flutter their wings and fly, as some of the apocryphal gospels would have us believe. Neither will we read in the gospel that our Lady, his mother, waited for angels to come and do the housework for her. Nor that Joseph had to engage in long arguments with the devil; nor that he spent every morning putting back together the carpentry tools which the devil had broken in pieces the night before.

One thing I want to say is this: the giddy child who could not be kept quiet at the age of three or four, who played with buttons, who swiped candy when no one was looking—that kid, like anyone else, can become a saint. But remember: in order to be saints we must be heroic human beings, mature persons. The canonized saints acquired this humanness, this human virtuousness, by making a steady effort; they weren't born with it. We, too, have to acquire it by a constant effort in prayer, in mortification, in everyday work.

How are we to become holy? Simply by loving the little things which we handle every day. What could be more encouraging or more consoling for our poor, struggling hearts?

RUPTURE BETWEEN LIFE AND RELIGION

I have said that the children of God no longer have any real desire to be saints. I tell you now that Christians have no clear idea of what Christianity is! It has not taken a firm hold on our lives; it has not been assimilated. There is still a terrible gap between the attitude we take toward our God when we're in church and the attitude we adopt toward our neighbor everywhere else. We think of Christ only when things go wrong. We lead, in fact, two lives: one life of work and another life of prayer, entirely distinct from one another; governed by completely different principles. The result is that our prayer is a great lie, and our work another great lie. We are trying to fight on two different fronts at the same time— a feat that the bravest soldier could not accomplish.

A lifeless faith, and a faithless life: are these not repulsive contradictions? What we understand is a Christianity of one hour a week—the Sunday obligation. We know nothing of that Christianity which ought to permeate our lives in all aspects, both private and public.

We understand easily enough the enthusiasm of Christians who go to daily Mass, but we find it difficult to realize that those same people ought to be exerting a healthy Catholic influence on the politics, the educational system, the media, and the economy of their country. The Christianity we understand is aloof from all social relations, isolated from the professions, confined to a person's thoughts and prayers. It's something to teach our children; it's a consolation to old people at the hour of death.

Those who do not know what loyalty is, or what dignity is, let them not try to march in the front lines. Let them be silent; let them hide themselves and not be seen.

Have you never come up against people who change their ideas according to the direction in which the wind happens to blow? That is certainly not Christianity. It was not for the purpose of teaching us ideas that Christ came down on earth. We mere mortals could easily have invented for ourselves that kind of religion. The Church, however, is God's invention. So, those who live their Catholicism only as a collection of private thoughts and feelings should never dare to call themselves Christian. The reality is that they're nothing but hypocrites and pietists who bring their silly, superficial frivolity even into their relations with God.

Perhaps you are under the impression that all pietists get up for Sunday Mass in the cold hours of the morning. Well, that's not so. Haven't you ever noticed how the regulars at the 10:30 Mass tend to laugh at the 8:00 Massgoers? The truth is that many people in both groups live a pseudo-piety that has no foundation. They have made the same mistake. With gigantic strength—the strength of the devil—they have shattered the essential unity of religion and life, the unity which brothers and sisters of ours lived perfectly in the early days of Christianity, when they were still warm with the breath of Christ's words.

The current chasm between religion and life is a result of that false piety which hides the truth from us Christians. The reason we lack the strength to win over the indifferent is that we have sundered the firm link which united the human and the divine, our life and the life of God. What I am trying to do in these pages is precisely this: to rouse you to unite with heaven the things of earth; to purify and sanctify them by your way of life.

There are many people who, when told that the love of God must be brought into the practical details of their lives, will answer, "I just want to get what I'm praying for; that's all I care about." How often we hear this from office workers worried by a business difficulty, or from students in the throes of examinations, from graduates seeking a good position, from homemakers in financial straits . . . from all sorts of people. What a narrow-minded way of looking at the relationship between ourselves and our Father-God. What an appalling rupture between religion and life!

❧ This is the means we must use to salvage the world before it falls to pieces: a unity of religion and life. Let us live every minute of our ordinary lives face to face with God. Let us make of our work a treasure in heaven, make of our sorrow a joy in heaven, make of our prayer a smile on the lips of Christ.

CHRISTIANS ARE NOT LIKE THAT

What a strange idea we have of our vocation as Christians! What a poor idea we have of those predecessors of ours who became saints: those truly human beings, individuals who were upright, stalwart, courageous, strong, clear of intellect, and clean of heart. Fearless souls! "I can do all things in him who strengthens me," says St. Paul (Phil 4: 13). And so can the rest of us. In the great work of the world, there will always be two working together: God, by means of his grace, and the individual cooperating with it generously, corresponding with it in complete harmony with God. We cannot separate the two, for God does not want to act alone, and any one of us if left alone would be helpless.

Remember, the Christian must represent the fullest development of our human nature. In other words, each of us must be authentically and completely human! Otherwise everything is useless and can lead only to dismal failure.

Christians must be in fact, as they are potentially, the first and most perfect of human beings.

But those creatures who escaped from God are approaching. I can hear their mournful voices. Out of the darkness there comes a chorus of despairing cries directed at the followers of Christ: "Show us by your *lives* that Christ is really alive!" I see them, their eyes clouded in darkness, their whole selves splashed with hatred, with blood; corpses craving for salvation, looking for God but finding only despair.

That unknown God they seek is our Christ! How often have we tried to tell them, but the truth always meets with the same old sardonic echo: "Only by your lives can you convince us that Christ is alive." We must speak the whole truth to those who have strayed from the Church, before their smoldering confidence in us is completely extinguished. Speak the truth to them; shout it at them. Before death plunges them into eternal sorrow, let them hear the truth at least once—the real truth. What they have seen in our religion up to now, blinded as they are by their own fury, is indeed a monstrosity. Our saints were not as they imagine them; that make-believe pietism of our times is not the sturdy piety that was preached by Christ twenty centuries ago. Tell them that now—at once.

No, forget that—tell them nothing! It is useless talking to them. The time has come to *act*. Let us act in silence, quietly, with discretion; but it is essential, it is vital, that we act effectively. By our fruits we shall be known. Let no one shirk the serious responsibility which rests upon the shoulders of each and every man, woman, and child baptized into the faith of Christ. The terrible thirst of those wretches who have trusted in leaking cisterns, cisterns which cannot hold water, needs much more today than the life of one saint. What the world needs now is a whole new generation of saints. Are you ready for action?

Take up the challenge of St. Josemaría: "Don't let your life be sterile. Be useful. Blaze a trail. Shine forth with the light of your faith and of your love. With your apostolic life wipe out the slimy and filthy mark left by the impure sowers of hatred. And light up all the ways of the earth with the fire of Christ that you carry in your heart." [6]

2. Human Maturity

IF THEY SEE SOME MAN WHOSE GOODNESS OF HEART AND CONDUCT HAVE WON THEIR RESPECT, THEY FALL SILENT AND STAND STILL.

—Virgil, *Aeneid*

PERSONALITY

BRETHREN, DO NOT BE CHILDREN IN YOUR THINKING; BE BABES IN EVIL, BUT IN THINKING BE MATURE.

—1 Corinthians 14:20

It was never my intention to write these pages in a negative or antagonistic tone. Actually, if you read them in a spirit of understanding, you will begin to assimilate and cherish a noble ideal. You will experience a heartfelt desire to come to grips with this great supernatural task, this gigantic task which we Christians have to do in this world. But you must admit that those who wish to construct anything of lasting value must first of all find a solid foundation on which to establish their work. Unfortunately so much of what we find is only shifting sand, or unsteady rubble, incapable of supporting the heavy weight of these critical days in which we live, and of the difficult times which lie ahead.

If we are to combat the enemies of the Church, we cannot put up with that cynical and sadistic pose they adopt. But neither can we excuse those who call themselves Christians and who live their Christianity in a shameful and careless manner. We cannot throw all the blame on "bad" people. We must examine our own consciences before rending our garments like the Pharisees.

We must be objective! If we will only open our eyes to reality we will see that one of the obstacles which Catholicism has to fight is the bad name which many so-called Catholics give the Church. It is of vital importance that we should win back for the word "Christianity" its true meaning. In the early days of the Church, Christians were people to be reckoned with. Today we are objects of pity. And believe me, one big reason for this sad truth is that so few of us are truly human.

We live in the world, and we must behave as true women and men of the world—though never in a worldly way. We must not be afraid to speak of personality simply because it is sometimes confused with vanity or pride; or of strength of character, which must always be distinguished from obstinacy; or of integrity, of will-power, of courage. These, among others, are virtues essential for every Christian.

You must not let anything frighten you. Real daughters and sons of Christ can be honored or martyred, but never despised. They leave a permanent imprint in the ground they tread. (One *must* leave a mark; otherwise one is no true son or daughter of Christ.) They give to their lives such a divine significance, they build it on such a divine foundation, that no human force can shake them.

If you hope to be a true Christian, you not only can but must develop a personality—your own individual personality. You are seriously obliged to do this. You must retain your own particular character, and your own mannerisms, without any artificial affectations. You must keep your own likes, your own dislikes, your own feelings. In short, you must keep everything that is human in you, provided that it is not a barrier between yourself and God.

Those individuals who have won the distinction of being included in the roster of the saints are all quite different; though there is a spirit common to them all, they each have unique features. To pour human beings into a mold to make all of them come out in the same shape would be—well, inhuman; extremely deformative. We should never try to do this to anyone, including ourselves. It would be childish and altogether abominable for us to try to copy the mannerisms or the behavior of the saints. We have been given only one name and one example to live by, and that is Christ. He alone has been set before us by the Creator for our emulation and therefore for our sanctification. So, "let each one test his own work, and then his reason to boast will be in himself alone and not in his neighbor. For each man will have to bear his own load" (Gal 6: 4–5).

Certainly we Christians must be known always and everywhere for our unity of spirit. This unity must be a source of edification and hope for those diseased and sickly souls who swarm all over the earth. This unity should also be a great encouragement to those stagnant souls who now look down on us with such disdain. "By this all men will know that you are my disciples, if you have love for one another" (Jn 13: 35). By this, and by your cheerfulness, and by your dignity and nobility of soul. But not by your homogeneity. Unity does not mean uniformity.

I cannot ignore the stupid mistake made by some people (for it is, indeed, a mistake) of trying to transform themselves, even in externals, into "typical" saints. The sorry result is that they, and perhaps those they direct, go about with eyes downcast and with their cheerful smile replaced by an unpleasant grimace. They no longer look you straight in the eye, as they once did. They are somehow changed, and not for the better—not entirely, anyway.

To make someone a saint, does grace have to destroy human nature? No, not at all. None of the essentials, none of the good qualities in human nature, need to be changed. To suppress any of one's good qualities—and there are always many—is the most deadly thing a Christian can do. Develop your character, your human faculties; develop them to the utmost degree. Anything that keeps you from growing, that limits your development, that makes you narrow-minded, that holds you back for fear of something, is not in any way Christian. The complete purification from sin and evil inclinations which, with the help of God, each of us has to accomplish does not involve suppressing any part of one's true personality. It is essential, it is vital, that you develop your personality to the full.

Although it is true that everyone is called to the kingdom of heaven, and that every person is capable of becoming a saint, it is ridiculous for us to let immature or incompetent persons run our affairs, however good or ostensibly good they may be. This poor idiot and that silly young fool have a place in our ranks; we cannot deny that. They are ill; they need the care due to sick persons. But they should never be allowed to occupy positions of responsibility. And yet they do occupy such positions, and that is one reason why our prestige is diminishing by the day.

We have every right to expect a Christian to achieve a more perfect development of personality, of purely human personality, than is possible for the non-Christian. It is important to recognize, however, that personality is not a form of pride. It is a basic constituent of humanness, something intrinsic to every individual. In fact, it is only with humility that you can fully develop your personality; you will only be fooling yourself if you think otherwise. At most you will attain a stock of stories, a wealth of verbiage, empty talk.

But do not let any of this frighten you. For now, simply see how much importance Pope Pius XII attached to personality and to personal effectiveness. In his address "The Catholic in Social Life," he says:

> You will never succeed in attracting the attention and the esteem of the man in the street by organization alone, no matter how perfect your organization may be, because his will be equal, if not superior, to yours. Bring then before his eyes the personality of the Catholic and the Christian beaming with joy who radiates all around him the living faith in which his heart abounds. Yes, in this manner it may well be that the man in the street may recover from his religious negligence and from his sloth of spirit, void of faith in God, and regain the feeling of his human dignity and his moral responsibility.[1]

You want to know whether you have true personality? Just ask yourself whether you are still yourself, your own natural self, when you are with others. Does the crowd overcome you? To win over the crowd—and that is precisely what you have to do—you can never be one of the crowd, though you must always be in the middle of it.

CHARACTER AND COURAGE

Saul, that famous persecutor of the Christians, is the absolute personification of rage and fury. The disciples of Christ are increasing and moving like wildfire all over the world, and if Saul is not careful they will end up overthrowing all his ideals. He cannot tolerate the Church; for him it is heresy. He has armed himself with complete civil power to bring about the death of those who, to his mind, are seeking the downfall of Judaism. So Saul "laid waste the Church, and entering house after house, he dragged off men and women and committed them to prison" (Acts 8:3). Saul is a source of terror to the Christians.

But God knows the loyalty of this creature of his, and he knows the principles which go to make up his character. So, to make him change his ways, God flings him violently from his horse. And Saul surrenders to God. The next few days he spends in silence, and recollection, and prayer. Days of light and strength; a complete interior revolution takes place. He sees now that those whom he has been persecuting are friends of God. By means of water and the Holy Spirit he ceases to be Saul the persecutor of Christians and becomes Paul the apostle.

With the very same energy as before, because he is the same man, the great Apostle of the Gentiles changes his ways and, with the dignity and valor of a noble soldier, sets out to preach the Truth which he has seen with his own eyes. Among the Christians there is astonishment, and among his friends, consternation. From that moment on, Paul is a man who puts all his energy, all his being, without the slightest reserve, into the service of Christ. He cheerfully accepts hunger, shipwreck, prison, fetters. He preaches in defense of those who worship the Lord, and does this without making himself a burden to anyone; he never stops subjecting himself to the hard work and fatigue of earning his living. In Christ he has seen the Way, the Truth, and the Life, and in his zeal to spread Christ's doctrine, he is determined never to rest until death ends his fruitful work. The cruel whip, vicious slander, iron chains, vile dishonor—nothing can ever separate him from his God.

Paul was a fearless person, and for that very reason he had the courage to surrender to God. Later on, also for that reason, he was always able to remain faithful to the principles of firmness, truth, and honor. I mention him to you as an example of a loyalty which is difficult to find in anyone today.

The life of Paul of Tarsus is most impressive. He is a man—and a saint—who fulfilled to the minutest detail all his obligations to society. And who, being a good citizen of his country, a citizen who always did his duty, also demanded all his rights. Perhaps you thought it was humility not to claim one's rights? Nonsense! Only those who do not fulfill their obligations should refrain from demanding their rights.

Paul does not go in for false humility. When he has a chance to escape the lashes of the whip, he does not remain silent and passively submit to the punishment. "But when they had tied him up with the thongs, Paul said to the centurion who was standing by, 'Is it lawful for you to scourge a man who is a Roman citizen, and uncondemned?' When the centurion heard that, he went to the tribune and said to him, 'What are you about to do? For this man is a Roman citizen.' So the tribune came and said to him, 'Tell me, are you a Roman citizen?' And he said, 'Yes.' The tribune answered, 'I bought this citizenship for a large sum.'" The tribune says this with a certain respect and fear. And Paul replies, outdoing himself in integrity, in human dignity, with the calm assurance of one who consciously lives the truth: "But I was born a citizen" (Acts 22: 25–28).

I want now to tell you a few more incidents from the life of this apostle, to let you see how a true Christian should behave in moments of difficulty.

False witnesses (see Acts 16: 19–37) testified against Paul and Silas, and by order of the magistrates, without any trial, they were stripped of their clothes and beaten with sticks in front of all the people. They were then thrown into prison—covered with wounds, closely guarded, their feet in chains. But they were happy to suffer for Christ. After some time the magistrates realized that they were innocent. The jailer entered their cell to release them in the name of justice: "The magistrates have sent to let you go; now therefore come out and go in peace." But no! A man like Paul, a real man, cannot tolerate such an insult. "They have beaten us, publicly uncondemned, men who are Roman citizens, and have thrown us into prison; and do they now cast us out secretly? No! Let them come themselves and take us out." That is the action of a man who could honestly say: "I always take pains to have a clear conscience toward God and toward men" (Acts 24: 16). You must admire the personality and courage of Paul, and the strength of his convictions.

If we want to be authentically Christian, we can never cease to be authentically human. To live, therefore, an interior life, a life of the soul, we can never give up being strong and vigorous. And the question now is why we have allowed this intimacy between our soul and our God, which should be a marvelous relationship, to become in so many cases enervated and insipid. Why have we allowed our interior life to become flabby? Why does it necessarily even have to be soft? That is, unfortunately, the mentality that has taken over. It seems as if all of us Christians have decided to forgo, as Christians, any and every masculine quality and to accept for our dealings with God, for our interior life, only forms and sentiments that are incompatible with a manly way of life. It is true, I suppose, that in general women have more inclination than men toward a life of affective devotion, more facility for religious practices rooted in "reasons of the heart." But that is no reason why men, who do, after all, have a psychology of their own, should allow themselves to be ruled by feminine psychology in their dealings with God. A man's interior life should, I am convinced, be founded on his reason and his will; it is unfortunate that so much of the time it suffers from an excess of unmanly sentiment.

One thing I can never understand is why every time a man speaks of interior life, he seems to feel obliged to use for his mode of expression—in his choice of words, his tone of voice, and so forth—a manner more appropriate to a woman than to a man. That is certainly not humility. You think these are mere questions of form? Unimportant trifles? Trifles, perhaps, but ones that are repugnant to any real man.

The first martyrs of that great transformation which Christ inaugurated were real men and women. But we never think of that because, quite frankly we are no longer Christians; we are flabby, miserable weaklings who have neither the strength nor the intelligence to put up a decent fight. Our crusaders of the Middle Ages were stouthearted warriors, full of human virtue. And Bernard, Dominic, Francis, Clare, Joan, Catherine—our saints of the Middle Ages—were strong and healthy men and women. So also were the confessors and virgins, the fathers and doctors, the martyrs of the early Church. So too were the saints of the past few centuries. So too are the saints of our own time, the ones living today side by side with us.

But in general the Christians of today know nothing of strength or courage. There may be a few brave souls among them, but the general atmosphere is one of flabbiness and feebleness. Catholics have become weak and cowardly. They shrink away from the noise of the world; they have lost contact with the people of the world, good or bad as these people may be; and they lead a lazy life of selfishness and comfort.

Nowadays we are inclined to confuse Christian charity

with lack of character. We calmly stand by while persons who are merely stupid are called good. We have too many holy Joes and too few Joes who are holy. Our complete lack of fortitude, our cowardliness, our absolute sterility in the matter of apostolate, all point to the fact that stupidity now passes for poverty of spirit and that we're expected to put up with it. We know nothing of that holy obstinacy, that refusal to compromise, that healthy personality which is so essential in a Christian life. Our weakness has made such inroads in our basic principles and in our external practices that our whole interior life, which should be vigorous and dynamic, is nothing but a tasteless mush, saccharine and clammy—a repulsive concoction! What one needs in order to be a soldier is courage! It's that simple.

What we need are strong, sturdy adults who are not afraid of pain, who can suffer in silence, who do not ask for sympathy. Adults who are not afraid of sacrifice, who do not shrink from conflict, who are fearless in the face of difficulties. Adults without fear of fear, who are not shy or selfish, who are never shocked by anything they see or hear. Maturity is courage. Energy and determination are not pride, they are essential components of a mature personality. True Christian men and women will never let themselves be trampled on, and they are ever ready to defend, with a strength which astounds the weaklings, the spirit and practices of the Christianity which they profess. Such courageous individuals have an upright bearing, noble gestures, a purposeful demeanor—none of the silly characteristics of a puppet. But you must never confuse mature character with mere obstinacy or bad manners.

If fortitude shows itself only sporadically on special occasions, then it is not a habit; and if it is to be a virtue, it must be a constant habit. True grit will show itself in the most insignificant details of our behavior—in, for example, the way we greet other people.

The Christians of today have to be exceptionally strong and healthy if generosity (a supernatural virtue essential to the undertaking of great enterprises) and high-mindedness (a supernatural virtue essential for overcoming great disappointments) are to develop in them, by means of grace, as fully as they did in the first Christians. You will never make anything really useful of a weakling who is afraid of a little cold water on a winter's morning!

But in a person of natural character, a person of courage, a person of strength, the infused virtue of fortitude will find a firm natural foundation, and the perfect union of natural virtue and supernatural virtue will make of that person a perfect soldier of Christ. So, you should rejoice and be happy when circumstances and people treat you badly. In such moments you should remember that God treats you thus because you are among the strongest of his daughters and sons. You say you find very little of that strength and vigor in those around you? Well, so what? Do you really want to be one of those, simply one of the crowd? If you do—if you want to go with the flow—then close this book. And while you're at it, you might as well close also, forever, that other book which contains the revolutionary credo of all rebellious Christians: the gospel. To you, if you are like this, and to other fools like you, all I can say is what the Florentine said: "Pass we on, nor waste our words." [2]

But if you are one of those (or if you at least wish to be one of those) who aspire to know God, to love him, to be happy with him, without leaving the busy world in which you live and work, then read on. To you, and to others like you, I say with St. Josemaría: "Be firm! Be strong! Be human! And then . . . be a saint!" [3]

LONGING FOR TRUTH

THE TRUTHS WHICH MEN IN ALL LANDS HAVE RIGHTLY SPOKEN
BELONG TO US CHRISTIANS.

— St. Justin Martyr, *Second Apology*

"I promise you." "I swear." "Word of honor." "I assure you." "Honestly." "It's the truth." How often we hear these emphatic phrases in the great marketplace of the world. In matters of business, and of love, we say them all the time. We always feel a great desire—more than a desire, a need—to convince others that we are speaking the truth. This goes on between parents and children, between best friends, between young lovers . . . Promises and oaths pledging our sincerity—and, underneath, vicious lies which destroy a person's whole life.

In this age we have lost all sense of shame. We habitually lie, completely conscious of what we're doing, out of spite, out of malice, out of evil passion. We tell lies—sometimes big, sometimes small—in public gatherings, in our family circles, in newspapers, on radio and television. We lie to those whom we call our friends, we lie to little children, we lie to God. And, sorry creatures that we are, we lie even to ourselves. Never before have individuals felt so alone and isolated among so many people.

"They bend their tongues like a bow; falsehood and not truth has grown strong in the land; for they proceed from evil to evil. . . . Let everyone beware of his neighbor, and put no trust in any brother; for every brother is a supplanter, and every neighbor goes about as a slanderer. Everyone deceives his neighbor, and no one speaks the truth; they have taught their tongue to speak lies" (Jer 9: 3–5). These lines still hold good for the present generation, for this world which is so old and which prides itself on being so advanced. Lying, of course, is nothing new. The father of all deceit is far older than the human race. He has been, ever since our world was young, darkening the hearts of miserable human beings and snatching their souls from the loving arms of the Father of all Truth.

It is the task of every Christian to save that same world, which is no longer young, from the confusion which is smothering it. Do you not feel the urgency, the vital necessity, of bringing the truth into every cave and cabin where humans live, of cleaning out the filth left behind by the doers of evil as they pass on their way through the world? How can you possibly remain calm and unmoved in the face of such a rampant epidemic of falsehood? Can it be that we sons and daughters of Truth are so degenerate, so listless, that we no longer make any effort to attain that truth, and even when we possess it we remain cold and indifferent? Are we to remain passive, like cowards, in the face of that terrible falsehood which surrounds us on all sides? God himself has provided us with the perfect contrast to the liars who are all around us. Paraphrasing a passage from the Book of Jeremiah (6: 27–30), I tell you that God has made us assayers of his gold to examine its value, and that, looking about us, we find only impure alloys and unwholesome mixtures. What comes out of very many mouths is neither gold nor silver, but only iron, lead, . . . metal which rings false.

Those who have fled from God are all now seeking that Truth which is the Way to reach eternal Life. Surely you are concerned about them? Precisely because they themselves are so steeped in falsehood and deceit, they are always glad to meet people who are truthful and well-balanced, who do not deceive themselves. And they are always watching our lives to see what kind of truth we are living. It is a universal fact that anything which is good in itself, and at the same time scarce, is greatly desired, and sought after, and appreciated. That is why the worldly yearn to know the truth.

We must not be surprised, then, if they are shocked to find that same worldly falsehood in many of us Christians.

What they seek is truth, sincerity, loyalty, nobility. In us they find little of these human virtues, because we have deformed the marvelous supernatural virtues by denying them their proper support, their essential foundation, their natural source of development, which is our human nature. Truth, nowadays, is relegated to the confessional; sincerity is reserved only for our petitions to God; loyalty is limited to the fulfillment of our devotions. As for nobility, we hardly know the meaning of the word.

The problem, as Dom Columba Marmion expresses it, is this:

> In order to act as Christians, we must first of all act as men. And this is not without importance. Doubtless, a perfect Christian will necessarily fulfill his duties as man, for the law of the gospel comprises and perfects the natural law. But one meets with Christians, or rather with some calling themselves Christians, and that not only among the simple faithful, but even among religious and priests, who are exact even to scrupulosity as to their self-chosen practices of piety, and yet hold certain precepts of the natural law very cheaply. These people have it at heart not to miss their exercises of devotion, and this is excellent, but, for example, they do not refrain from attacking a neighbor's reputation, from telling falsehoods, and from failing to keep their word; they do not scruple to give a wrong meaning to what an author has written nor to infringe the laws of literary or artistic

property; they defer, sometimes to the detriment of justice, the payment of their debts, and are not exact in observing the clauses of a contract.[4]

And Jacques Bossuet says something similar:

One is uneasy if he has not said his rosary or other fixed prayers, or if he has omitted some *Ave Maria* in a decade; I do not blame him; God forbid! I have only praise for religious exactitude in exercises of piety. But who can endure to have this same person easily breaking four or five precepts of the Decalogue daily without troubling, and treading underfoot the holiest duties of Christianity without scruple?[5]

I have told you once, and I will tell you again: it is impossible for Christians to lead two lives, one for dealings with God and a different one for dealings with people. We must adopt one and the same attitude toward religion and toward our ordinary life, since they are as intimately united with each other as the soul is with the body. Any other outlook is false and contemptible. And that is why we see so many false and contemptible lives all around us.

One of the key factors in the historical development of the human race is our sense of truth. Truth in a human being is a conformity between what should be and what in fact is. Therefore, the less human you are, the further you will be from truth. And the more human you are, the nearer you will be to Christ, who is Truth itself.

Are we, then, to go on despising those human virtues which some people erroneously call "exterior" virtues? Actually they are so interior, so very intimate, that they go to the very root of our nature and are intrinsic parts of our whole being. Everything we do, if it is to be truthful, must be done in complete conformity with our human nature; any action outside this line of conduct is false, and therefore meaningless. And when that falsehood is exercised knowingly and with the intention of deceiving, then it is a lie.

"[Holy Father,] sanctify them in the truth; thy word is truth" (Jn 17: 17). O Lord, make us humanly truthful so that people may follow us and come closer to you! There is, indeed, much truth in the world, but how much more in evidence, more common, more apparently normal, is deceit!

If we were in absolute conformity with our nature, we would be all truth! Make us human, O Lord, that we may become holy! That liberating truth, that life-giving truth, will motivate us to traverse all the ways on the face of the earth—ways that stretch far ahead—with our heads held high, a smile on our faces, our spirits cheerful, and in our hearts a flaming desire to lay at the feet of Christ those miserable souls enchained by the father of lies.

To pagans, and to people of little faith, I say this: The truth will set you free! Seek it now, before night and darkness come and blind you forever. We who are Christians, who are really Christians, hold the secret of that peace which you seek. Outside of Christ you will never find it.

And to all faith-filled Christians I say this: Never fear those wretches who are groping about in search of truth. Love them. The true Christian, realizing that he or she possesses by faith what others seek through their own efforts, leaves the way open for them to find that truth. More than that: the true Christian will actively encourage the sincere efforts of the pagan scientist, of the unbelieving news reporter, of the faithless politician, of the atheist researcher, all of whom may be trying with all their might to demolish something that we know is built on an immovable foundation. Let them search! Let them work! We have nothing to fear. We have the truth. All truth is one, and all truth is in our Lord. We have the truth, and we must live the truth so that Christ's praise of Nathanael may be extended to us all:

> "Behold, an Israelite indeed, in whom is no guile!" (Jn 1:47).

THE NATURAL AND THE SUPERNATURAL

EVEN IN SANCTITY, EVEN IN GRACE, MAN CANNOT REALIZE HIS HIGHER VOCATION UNLESS HE TAKES THE FACT OF HIS HUMANITY SERIOUSLY, AND THAT WITHOUT RESERVATION. THIS TRUTH HOLDS GOOD IN REGARD TO ALL THE . . . RELATIONSHIPS HE ESTABLISHES, BE IT WITH THE LOGOS, WITH ETHICS, WITH THE FACT OF MYSTERY, OR WITH THE WORKING VALUES OF THIS WORLD.

— Josef Sellmair, *The Priest in the World*

A strong personality, a truly human personality, is achieved by development of those human virtues which we received in an undeveloped form, as part of our nature, at conception. Two of the principal faculties which are characteristic of human beings, which distinguish us from the animals, are intelligence and free will. By the proper use of these two faculties, which are the sources and guiding principles of all truly human actions, a person must develop loyalty, honesty, endurance, a spirit of hard work, fraternal love, generosity, courage, cheerfulness, optimism, sincerity, sociability, . . . and, fundamentally those four human virtues—straight thinking, equity, courage, and self-control—on which are based the cardinal virtues.

A human being, by nature, necessarily tends toward a perfection based on the concrete fact of being human. One is more of a human being according as the human virtues are more deeply rooted in one's nature; and these take root only by way of repeated acts and personal efforts. Theoretically, in fact, to become a perfect human being need not entail any supernatural aid; the means provided by nature are sufficient.

In practice, however, anyone who tries to do without grace and attain that ideal by purely natural means, by his own natural strength, will become no more and no less than an animal. Father Garrigou-Lagrange explains:

> As long as a man remains in the state of mortal sin, these true virtues remain in the state of a somewhat unstable disposition (*in statu dispositionis facile mobilis*); they are not yet in the state of solid virtue (*difficile mobilis*). Why is this? The answer is that as long as a man is in the state of mortal sin, his will is habitually turned away from God. Instead of loving Him above all else, the sinner loves himself more than God, with the consequent result that he shows great weakness in accomplishing moral good, even of the natural order.[6]
>
> Because of mortal sin, the will is turned directly away from the supernatural last end, and indirectly from the natural last end, for the natural law itself obliges us to obey God, no matter what He may command. Thus every sin against the supernatural last end is indirectly a sin against the natural law.[7]
>
> The true acquired virtues which are in a man in the state of mortal sin lack solidity because they are not connected, because they are not sufficiently supported by the closely related moral virtues that are often lacking.[8]
>
> That true acquired virtues may not be simply in a state of unstable disposition, and that they may be in a state of solid virtue (*in statu virtutis*), they must be connected. That this may be so, a man must no longer be in the state of mortal sin, but his will must be set straight in regard to his last end. He must love God more than himself, at least with a real and efficacious

> love of esteem, if not with a love that is felt. This love
> is impossible without the state of grace and without
> charity.[9]

Just as our conception makes us human by giving us
this nature, inherent in which are the seeds of certain
human virtues, in the same way the sacrament of Baptism makes us Christian by giving us grace, and with it,
in an embryonic form, the infused theological and moral
virtues and the gifts of the Holy Spirit, all of which are
essential for achieving the supernatural end for which we
are destined.[10]

Baptism produced in our souls a radical change.
Through original sin we were born, to some extent, as
objects of the divine anger; now we are daughters and
sons of God. In one moment we were transformed,
through grace, from sin-enslaved rational animals to
beings that are superior to what the angels themselves,
by their nature, can claim to be. God has made us members of his own race.

Since we are now, through grace, children of God, we
must be careful always to act in a way proper to children
of such a great king. And to enable us so to act, God our
Father has directly placed in our souls the necessary
strength: the infused virtues. These are called "supernatural" because they are above the requirements of nature.
Some of them are also called "theological," because they
are related to God directly; he is their immediate object.
To believe in God and in all that God has revealed, to
desire to possess God himself, to love him more than our
very lives—these are faith, hope, and charity. Others of
these virtues are called "moral," their immediate object
being the supernatural *means* which are necessary in
order for us to attain our supernatural end. Prudence,
justice, fortitude, and temperance together form the base
of a whole pyramid of virtues which we have to practice

if the priceless treasure we have, a personal relationship with God himself, is not to be lost through mortal sin or tainted through venial sin.

Through the grace of God we are God's sons and daughters. Through the infused virtues we are capable of acting as such. But all that is not sufficient. In spite of everything we have received from God, we are still creatures in a fallen world; we carry on our shoulders the heavy weight of the fallout of original sin. Our reason is still liable to error, and it can never know, anyway, because it is very limited, all that it would like to know.[11] Sometimes we behave in a worthy manner, because our reason reigns over our appetites and our senses; at other times we act like imbeciles, because we let our senses control us. It is essential that the Holy Spirit should not leave us alone in the struggle which we have to go through to achieve that union with Christ, that union in sanctity, which is our goal. And the Spirit of God has not neglected this vital concern. The Spirit gives us inspirations so that we can easily advance toward our perfection. The dispositions which make of a person a docile and pliable subject of divine inspiration are called the "gifts of the Holy Spirit." There you have an overview of the whole supernatural organism which God infused into your soul when you were baptized with water from our earthly streams.

From the moment of your baptism onward, the only important thing, the only thing that really matters, the thing which is to decide your eternal destiny, is unquestionably that *state of grace* which God has given you. However mature you may be in terms of human virtues, never for one moment forget that if you die in mortal sin you will go to hell—with all your human virtues.

We rely, therefore, on the grace of the sacraments in order to live as Christians. There you have it. That is the way; never lose sight of it. Faith, hope, charity: essential. Prudence, justice, fortitude, temperance: indispensable. Prayer, sacrifice: vital. Communion of saints, spiritual childhood: absolutely necessary. Who is the liar who denies any of this? Who is the fool who conceals or forgets it?

Are you surprised now because in all of this I haven't spoken of our Lady? There actually was a fellow who said of the first edition[12] of this "arrogant" little book that he did not understand why I failed to mention any saints who attained sanctity by means of the rosary, or any who reached heaven by means of spiritual exercises. Well, did he think this book was meant to be a showcase of our finest gems?

What I want to emphasize is the fact that these supernatural virtues which came to us directly from God, these virtues which are divine in essence, have to be developed in us—in you and in me and in all Christians—on the basis of the human nature which we received at conception. The supernatural organism should be grafted onto a strong and healthy organism of human virtues.

I want you to develop your human virtues to the full, because Christ, our model, did exactly that.

Christ was humanly perfect. He was the human being *par excellence*. Christ acted always with the maximum material perfection. "He has done all things well" (Mk 7: 37). Christ possessed all the human virtues, in full measure.

For all of us, then, the necessity of those virtues acquires a very special significance. Christ, who had a human nature which was perfect, totally free from sin, found no obstacle to the practice of the virtues. And we find so many! The development of the moral virtues (humility, gentleness, piety, patience, obedience, chastity, penance), as well as that of the cardinal virtues, is impeded by many serious obstacles in our human nature.

Dom Marmion succinctly outlines both the problem and the solution. "There are within us," he says, "depraved inclinations resulting from atavism and temperament, as well as from the bad habits we contract, which are so many obstacles to the perfect fulfillment of the divine will. What is to remove these obstacles? The infused moral virtues that God places in us with grace? No, they have not, of themselves, this privilege. Undoubtedly they are admirable principles of operation; but it is a psychological law that the destruction of vicious habits and the redressing of evil inclinations can be effaced only by the contrary habits, and these good habits themselves result only from the repetition of acts: thence the acquired moral virtues." [13]

The human virtues—called "acquired" virtues because they are exclusively the fruit of a repetition of human acts and personal efforts [14]—are the walls flanking a great canal; they are the watertight bulwarks which prevent the sides from falling in under the pressure from all around. On the bed of the canal the divine waters of grace can then flow easily, with no obstacles of the flesh to impede the flow.

The infused moral virtues form a supernatural lining for those sturdy walls built by human effort, so that charity can flow freely and with profit to the soul.

When these bulwarks are lacking, when one makes no effort to channel the water, then grace meets only obstacles in the soul, and only a miracle can get rid of those obstacles. But, my friend, God will not work miracles to help a soul which does nothing for God.

What good can the infused virtue of fortitude do in a soul which knows nothing of the human virtue of courage? If the basis for fortitude is lacking, the very law of gravity makes it crumble and fall to dust among the cracks and crevices of that cowardly soul.

How can the supernatural virtue of magnanimity thrive in a person who is on the natural level narrow-minded and fainthearted, who shirks any great undertaking for fear of the effort involved?

How can a mediocre drifter acquire a spirit of Christian mortification?

How can generosity prosper in a selfish soul which limits everything to its own petty interests?

It is true, as Dom Marmion says, that in certain cases the theological virtue of charity can engender, so to speak, the acquired moral virtues; inspired by love, a person can begin, little by little, to practice acts which, given enough repetition, will eventually produce the corresponding virtues.[15] "If you love me, you will keep my commandments" (Jn 14: 15). But that will happen only in special cases, and only in persons who are very advanced in the divine life. For us, for you and for me, the old phrase holds good: God helps those who help themselves.

"It is inconceivable," says Father Josef Sellmair, "that the . . . supernatural virtues should be lively and real if the natural virtues remain unpracticed." [16] And says St. Francis de Sales: "In whatever regards our perfection, which consists in the union of our soul with the divine goodness, it is not so much a question of knowing as of doing much." [17]

In short, the necessity of the human moral virtues is something that should be obvious and unquestionable. They facilitate extrinsically the practice of the supernatural virtues, affecting the infused moral virtues directly and the theological virtue of charity indirectly (because charity needs the support of the moral virtues for its full development).

I have told you that to be Christian you must first of all be human. I want to end this section by saying something about the other side of this coin: namely, that under the powerful influence of love, all these human virtues which you possess will become the basis, the dominating principle, the springboard, of countless acts which will merit for you eternal life.

You know that you must "love God with all your heart, with all your soul, with all your mind, with all your strength" (Mk 12: 30). That is the first great commandment. No human action whatsoever is excluded from the sphere of grace, of charity, of merit. "Whatever you do, in word or deed, do everything in the name of the Lord Jesus, giving thanks to God the Father through him" (Col 3: 17). "Whether you eat or drink, or whatever you do, do all to the glory of God" (1 Cor 10: 31).

Your work and your play, your most enjoyable activities and onerous tasks, the most ordinary, the most commonplace, the most trivial actions of your life: do them all for the glory of God. No honest activity is excluded from Christian life. If only you want to, you can saturate every effort, every sacrifice, every tear, with the powerful influence of God's grace. If you act always in this manner, in the state of grace and with a right intention, then all your human virtues, everything you do in any capacity, will come within the wonderful range of the activity of the daughters and sons of God. Grace does not create human activity. What it does do is supernaturalize already existing activities; it sanctifies and makes supernatural in a formal way all human actions which are done with a right intention. When a work is accomplished on a natural plane, we can be sure that with and through grace, it is accomplished on the supernatural level, as well. And this fact is the foundation for the sanctification of our ordinary lives.

Do you not see the potential magnificence and perfect simplicity of the ordinary life of every Christian? But you must not get the idea that to achieve this magnificence and simplicity, all one has to do is collaborate with God in some hazy or indefinite way. Something much more is necessary: namely, the cooperation of our nature with God's grace, of the human virtues with the supernatural, of the body with the soul, of life with religion—in a word, the collaboration of the human element with the divine. It is from a fusion of your natural self with Christ, the Word made flesh, that the saint will emerge.

When the grace of God finds the natural faculties well developed in a person—the faculties of intelligence, of will-power, of courage, of sensitivity, of imagination—it instills life into them in such a way that it makes of that Christian a much more worthy saint, of more value to God and benefit to the world, than if that person had none of those faculties. The most striking example I can think of is St. Paul.

The mysteries of grace being infinitely deep and wonderful, we can never hope to estimate the part played by human souls in the redemption of the human race. But what I can tell you is that today's world needs Christians who have strong, forceful personalities and who are conscious of the fact (since humility is truth) that they have a duty to put themselves at the service of God with everything in them—with all their energy, with all the talents which the Lord has entrusted to them. Whoever buries his talents in the sand will merit from God nothing but contempt.

I quote you the words of Pope Pius XII: "Each one of the faithful and every man of good will must re-examine, with a courage worthy of the great moments of human history, what he can and must do personally, as his own contribution to the saving power of God, in order to help a world which, today, has set foot on the road to ruin." [18]

But there are still some people, and there always will be, who get nervous when someone writes, as I am writing now, that it is "I" and not simply "each one of the faithful" who in the final analysis will have to do the work. If we always take refuge in the anonymous third person, it will seem that we lack individuality.

SOLDIERS OF CHRIST

IF THERE IS A PROPHET AMONG YOU, I THE LORD MAKE MYSELF KNOWN TO HIM IN A VISION, I SPEAK WITH HIM IN A DREAM. NOT SO WITH MY SERVANT MOSES; HE IS ENTRUSTED WITH ALL MY HOUSE.

— Numbers 12: 6–7

In the following pages I want to show those people who look down on us Christians derisively, or contemptuously, or pityingly, that there is a marvelous human dignity and greatness in being a soldier of Christ. And I want to call to the attention of you believers a few of the problems which face the Christian of today, and the solutions to those problems, so that you will have the motivation and the strength to cast far from you that attachment to senseless routine which is holding you down. I want to encourage you to live for Christ, with Christ, and in Christ an energetic life which will counteract the inertia of the indifferent masses.

I feel sorrow and even some fear for the future when I think of the false ideas so many people have of our saints. They are always being classified among the characters of legend and fable, or relegated to the histories of centuries long past. They are always placed very low down, far below the rest of the population, in caves, away from the noise of big cities; or else very high up, far above other mortals, above the clouds; always very far away from everybody else.

But the reality is startlingly different. Our saints actually live very near us, right beside you and me. At this very moment, as you are reading this book, there are saints reading this same book with you; that is how close they are. The only thing is, sanctity does not always show externally.

I am not speaking now of superheroes, but of ordinary Christians. It could be somebody who works with you in the lab; who sits right next to you in class or at the office; who serves you behind the counter; who gives you a seat on the bus . . . simply one or more of your companions in the hard work of every day.

That is the way soldiers of Christ behave on the outside. We have said it before: there is nothing, no mark or exterior sign of any kind, to distinguish them from other people. But inside they are women and men full of faith, of hope, of love; burning with faith, burning with hope, burning with love.

Do not think that the soldiers of Christ are incapable of sinning. Every saint, every Christian, every one of God's creatures in this fallen world will have defects. Nevertheless, the saints make use of their human nature; they make use of it to achieve a real union with God in this life. They know, of course, that they will achieve perfection only after death—after a death which is nothing other than the change from imperfect to perfect, from war to peace, from temporality to eternity, from the discontinuous Eucharist on this earth to the perpetual Eucharist in heaven. I should like you to study the defects of the saints, and the means they took and the efforts they made to overcome those defects. It would help you to see that they were quite human, quite ordinary individuals.

Christ never knew sin. Our Mother in heaven never knew sin. But everyone else, all the saints, had the same human defects you and I have. Those "lives of the saints" which give one the impression that the saints were virtually faultless, and that sanctity is reserved for a certain privileged few, are pernicious documents that may well be responsible for the warping of many Christian consciences. That false idea must be avoided. It contradicts the truth, shown so clearly in the Gospels, that "Be perfect" is meant for every one of us.

Anyone can achieve perfection! There is no human occupation (barring those that are inherently sinful) in which one cannot achieve sanctity. The theater, the cinema, art, the press, law (though my experience in this last profession left me convinced that lawyers have to tread a very narrow path in order to be saved!)—none of these can be excluded from the means of achieving sanctity. We have several examples of movie stars and other celebrities who "left the world" and became perfect. Trust in God and wait but a little while, and you will see others who do not abandon those same professions and who go straight from this earth to heaven. And then the Church, Mother of all Christians, will point to their lives as examples for us to follow. Just wait and see!

I once came across a sentence that it still pains me to read: "Catastrophes, wars, economic crises, cannot prevent saints from becoming holy, poets from writing, artists from painting, scholars from studying." Because it pains me so much, I do not wish to give the source. As if sanctity were merely one job among others—poets write, and saints become holy! Who ever heard of the profession of "saint"? It is true that the Church recognizes certain lifestyles as "states of perfection," but we are speaking here of the majority of Catholics—in other words, lay people. There aren't any men or women whose job it is to become saints *instead of* studying, or ploughing, or making a home, or writing poetry. Such either/or thinking is nonsense! It is the poets, the artists, the farmers, the homemakers, the students, the professors, the domestics, who become saints, and they become saints precisely in, and by means of, their poetry, their art, their fields, their families, their books, the floors they scrub, the dishes they wash.

The biographies of great individuals usually emphasize their great actions, the heroic acts they performed on a few spectacular days, a few glorious points in their lives. I should like to read not so much about those isolated events, but more about their ordinary behavior on all the days which went before, in order to discover whether that great hour emphasized so much by their biographers was one isolated hour, an aberration in their lives, in which case there is very little to admire in it, or whether it was the logical result of the heroic way they lived out all the monotonous days of their ordinary lives. I should like details not about the spectacular deeds of the soldier who was on guard when the crater of Vesuvius erupted, but about the way he behaved when he was on guard the day before.

In order to get to know ourselves, we must retreat into silence. Life is too hectic; we must relax a little. Otherwise we will never see ourselves as we really are. We must not be afraid of finding that we are imperfect— we already know that anyway. Rather, we must try to discover the gifts and the talents placed in us by God.

An examination of conscience that is purely negative—a list of faults—will get us nowhere. It can only lead to a ridiculous superficial humility, one that is pessimistic and fruitless, and, consequently, to an annihilation of our natural, as well as supernatural, life, to a total aloofness, to an indifference unworthy of a human being.

If we want to be Christian, we must choose the way of struggle, of strength, of courage. We must know not only the bad, but also something of the good inclinations which we possess, recognizing that not everything in our nature is evil. We must know especially those qualities, those divine values, which God has placed in our intelligence, in our mouth, in our heart, in our deeds, in our temperament, in our character. God, who never does anything without a reason, placed in us the seeds of many virtues, and it is our job to develop and cultivate them. Thus, some of us will be brave by nature, others will be cheerful, others will be generous, others will be hard-working. But we must all try to develop whatever virtues do not come naturally to us, as well as those that do.

Keep your eyes open. Get to know yourself. Remember, the one with five talents will be expected to give back another five talents. And those of us who have only one talent cannot get by with hiding it in the sand out of fear of our Lord. Look back for a moment, over the years. What do you see? A poor life; a very poor life. Up to now you have done practically nothing. But trust in the word of God, and the miracle will happen.

By one good confession the sins of past years are all blotted out. A little mortification will dispel the murky shadows that remain. Then look ahead. Look at the path that has yet to be trodden—at the new ways to be explored; ways on which, apparently, no human has set foot before. Yes, the early Christians passed along some of them, but the silent years have covered their tracks with weeds.

Be constant in your resolutions. Be constant in the work you have to do today, wherever you are, whatever you have to do. Learn to love your work, whatever it is.

Be jealous of no one, Christian or non-Christian. Remind yourself often that it is to God himself that you will have to give an account of your talents. Why be jealous of anyone or anything? You have at your finger-tips all the means you need for becoming a saint, for doing great work in the world. Persevere in the job you have to do today; persevere in your work.

Raise your eyes to the Lord, look him straight in the eye, and you will learn to love him. And then, when you are full of God, you will find it very easy to live in a supernatural manner the human virtues in your person-ality. You will live them with great simplicity, day after day, with a supernatural naturalness. If you have to be hard on yourself, to treat yourself roughly, do not shirk that responsibility. Don't let it worry you. Do not think it paradoxical when I tell you that it is precisely then, when you have to fight against the base tendencies of your human nature, that you are being most human. It is then that your natural virtues, lived in a supernatural manner, will form a strong antithesis to, and barrier against, those vices which nauseate all those who are not content to be anything less than soldiers of Christ:

> against falsehood, truthfulness;
> against pettiness, nobility;
> against hypocrisy, sincerity;
> against superficial pietism, real piety;
> against weakness, strength;
> against affectation, simplicity;
> against narrow-mindedness, daring;
> against inconstancy, endurance;
> against cowardice, courage;
> against treachery, loyalty;
> against downheartedness, cheerfulness;
> against pessimism, optimism;
> against insipidity, personality;
> against laziness, diligence;

against disorderliness, orderliness;
against miserliness, generosity;
against talkativeness, reserve;
against showiness, discretion;
against mediocrity, sanctity.

And then, on the last day, your Father-God will say to you: "I remember the devotion of your youth, your love as a bride, how you followed me in the wilderness, in a land not sown" (Jer 2: 2).

Cherish from the start the blessed conviction that everything is possible. How sad it is to hear so many souls empty of love say that it is too much, that we could never persevere. Of course we can. We will repeat this to them throughout our lives: that it is easy, quite easy. All we have to do is learn to love God.

3. THE WHIP

A MAN—A "GENTLEMAN"—READY TO COMPROMISE WOULD CONDEMN
JESUS TO DEATH AGAIN.

— St. Josemaría Escrivà, *The Way*, no. 393

It is indisputable that we Christians must be very under-standing of other people's defects, of their different tem-peraments, of their various characters. This holds true as concerns our friends, our enemies, everyone. We must be patient in the face of personal insult when it hurts our pride, when it impugns our honor, when it destroys our good name, when it ruins our chances in life. Such treat-ment helps to form and develop us; it helps us to control our pride. In short, it purifies us. In all those things we must give way, forgive, yield. But that is not what I mean by "compromise."

Are we to give way in a matter of doctrine at the expense of truth? Never!

Are we to compromise in a manner that could harm the Church? Never!

Nor in anything else which relates directly to God. We must have understanding and forgiveness for the ignorant and the sick, but for "goodish" people, never! You think what is needed here is tolerance? Nonsense!

You say we must tolerate error? Rubbish!

Surely you agree that a mother's name must be respected whenever her son is present. Well, then, how can any Christian man stand by quietly when someone speaks disrespectfully of the Church, his mother?

I never ask Christians to make an outward show of their interior life of piety; there is no need for that. But I do ask of you, I demand of you, that you should be ready at any moment to defend your religion with the last drop of your Christian blood.

You think a willingness to compromise is a sign of humility? It is nothing of the kind; it has no relation at all to humility. It is often mere cowardice, and it is often ignorance. If we love truth, if we even want to love truth, we must learn to defend it against all attack. And if we do not love the truth, it is because we are ignorant of its enormous life-giving powers. No one who loves truth, who lives truth, will ever remain passively tolerant while others ridicule its solid foundations. The knowledge of truth gives one strength; it gives one the dynamism that one needs in order to keep aiming at sanctity and not be scared off by the difficulties that come up along the way. If you allow yourself to be carried away by the currents of public opinion, you are showing that you have a weak personality, that you are merely one of the crowd, that you are willing to tolerate anything that does not directly affect your own pride or personal interests.

READINESS TO FIGHT

People who always give in, who are always ready to compromise, to take the easy way out, to please everyone at any cost—those, in other words, whose faith has no deep or firm roots—would quietly stand by and see Christ crucified all over again.

They would watch once again, "impartially," that dreadful scene. They would "open-mindedly" listen to the curses and jeers of the mob who spat in the face of the Ever-Holy; they would nonchalantly tolerate the insults of the hordes, the vile utterances of the crowd. In fact, some of them would willingly nail him to the wood, more energetically than the Roman soldiers did; with sharper nails that would eat into his flesh and shatter every bone in his body. They would gladly keep watch over the tomb, wide awake, eyes blazing with frenzy. There would be no danger of sleep overcoming their hatred.

On one occasion some of the Pharisees came to Jesus and said to him, "Get away from here, for Herod wants to kill you." And he said to them, "Go and tell that fox, 'Behold, I cast out demons and perform cures today and tomorrow, and the third day I finish my course'" (Lk 13: 31–32). Christ would not let himself be killed until his hour came, just as Paul would not submit to being whipped by the Romans (see Acts 22).

Our hearts are on fire, O Lord, with love for you and with zeal for your house. We desire to be sincerely passionate for truth, the most sincere and the most passionate people that the earth has known. We ask you for that zeal, O Lord, with all the humility which poor Peter lacked at the Last Supper.

We must always love and admire the flowing blood of the early martyrs. That blood confirmed us in our faith. We reverence it because it brought us life. But we realize, O Lord, that martyrdom is too valuable a prize for the misery in which we are sunk at this moment. If you were to grant it to us, we would kiss your feet in thanksgiving. We would trust in you to give us the strength to stand up to the attack of the wild beasts, and to spring lightly from these shadows in which we live into that Light which is never dimmed. But the vocation given to us Christians of today is not to be martyrs, but to be warriors.

I am not saying that because we, as members of the Catholic Church, have access to the fullness of God's revealed truth, we should be hard on those who do not.

But I am saying that because we have been blessed with the truth, we must be ready to defend it against anyone who dares to disparage or ridicule it. If the enemies of the Church think that they are going to find in Catholicism weak or sickly spirits who will resignedly raise their hands in defeat at the first sign of attack and simply let the Church be run to the ground, they are very much mistaken.

THE FIRST BOOK OF THE MACCABEES

Every Christian, every one of you who remain faithful to Christ by living in humility and gentleness, by having love for your enemies, by allowing no place in your heart for bitterness or vengefulness, by being the most understanding of all people, must take up a warrior's weapons—arms of defense and attack—wherever the Church of God is in danger. You must meet enemies of the Church on their own ground; you must answer them with the same weapons they use to attack the Church. It may be on an intellectual field; in such a case you must answer with your own professional expertise. But if the attack is a bloody one, or a fiery one, then with blood and fire you must respond. Otherwise you cannot speak to me of your humility, or of your gentleness. Those would then be only false virtues covering up a shameful cowardice.

I want to give you as an example the Maccabees, to show you how you should behave when the forces of Satan break loose from hell and rise against the children of God. (All Scripture references in this section are from 1 Maccabees.)

> The king [Antiochus] wrote to his whole kingdom that all should be one people, and that each should give up his customs. All the Gentiles accepted the command of the king. Many even from Israel gladly

adopted his religion; they sacrificed to idols and profaned the sabbath. And the king sent letters by messengers to Jerusalem and the cities of Judah; he directed them to follow customs strange to the land, to forbid burnt offerings and sacrifices and drink offerings in the sanctuary, to profane sabbaths and feasts, to defile the sanctuary and the priests, to build altars and sacred precincts and shrines for idols, to sacrifice swine and unclean animals, and to leave their sons uncircumcised. They were to make themselves abominable by everything unclean and profane, so that they should forget the law and change all the ordinances. "And whoever does not obey the command of the king shall die" (1:41–50).

Pride, arrogance, the thirst for power, inevitably make of such a king a poor devil in the hands of Satan, a pygmy in rebellion against the divine law. By order of this tyrant, the temple in Jerusalem was consecrated to Zeus, and, in every village in the country, idols were set up for the purpose of obliterating the name of Yahweh. One such town was Modein, and envoys of the king arrived there, as elsewhere, to enforce the royal decree. This town had an outstanding leader, named Mattathias. Naturally the commissioners went first to him so that his example might convince his relatives and friends. The reward offered was cunning and tempting: "You and your sons will be numbered among the friends of the king, and you and your sons will be honored with silver and gold and many gifts" (2:18). Whatever reply this man gave, by word or by deed, it would set the standard for the rest of the town. There had to be one person to direct the others in what seemed to be this inescapable dilemma: either to abandon the law of God or else to die.

Even nowadays people tend to think that in such cases there are only these two alternatives, that everyone must adopt the one attitude or the other. But that is not true!

One can never right an injustice by shrugging one's shoulders and resigning oneself to it. One rights an injustice only by imposing justice! In such cases there is a third possible attitude: the courageous attitude, the attitude adopted by Mattathias.

> But Mattathias answered and said in a loud voice: "Even if all the nations that live under the rule of the king obey him, and have chosen to do his commandments, departing each one from the religion of his fathers, yet I and my sons and my brothers will live by the covenant of our fathers. Far be it from us to desert the law and the ordinances. We will not obey the king's words by turning aside from our religion to the right hand or to the left" (2: 19–22).

But not all the townspeople were strong and courageous. There were plenty of weaklings who were quite willing to serve their God when the obligations he imposed were easy to fulfill, but who were slow to serve when that service might be stained in blood. These people were soon to see that Mattathias' declaration of war was no idle threat.

> When he had finished speaking these words, a Jew came forward in the sight of all to offer sacrifice upon the altar in Modein, according to the king's command. When Mattathias saw it, he burned with zeal and his heart was stirred. He gave vent to righteous anger; he ran and killed him upon the altar. At the same time he killed the king's officer who was forcing them to sacrifice, and he tore down the altar. Thus he burned with zeal for the law, as Phinehas did against Zimri the son of Salu (2: 2–26).

The rebellion of those who would worship only one God had begun. The chosen people of Yahweh, in spite of all the errors and meanderings they had made in the course of their history, had managed to remain fundamentally true to their monotheism, basically resistant to the polytheistic influences of the neighboring peoples. That was the whole purpose of their being chosen, and Israel, ultimately, was faithful to her promise. The courageous voice of Mattathias was heard in every corner of that land of prophets and of kings, and the filthy bellies of the lifeless gods shuddered in fear. "Let everyone who is zealous for the law and supports the covenant come out with me!" (2:27). They left in the city everything they had, and took refuge in the mountains—whole families, along with their herds . . . Some of them went into hiding in the desert.

The forces of King Antiochus began the terrible persecution. They were, of course, acquainted with the customs of the rebels, so they decided to attack on the sabbath, the day on which all observers of the law were obliged to rest and remain in one place. In order not to profane the obligatory rest, those who had taken refuge in the desert never lifted a stone to fling at their attackers; they did not even try to prevent the enemies from entering their caves. "So, they attacked them on the sabbath, and they died, with their wives and children and cattle, to the number of a thousand persons" (2:38).

Mattathias (who was a priest) and his friends heard of this incident, and were sorely grieved at the attitude taken by their friends. "Each said to his neighbor: 'If we all do as our brethren have done and refuse to fight with the Gentiles for our lives and our ordinances, they will quickly destroy us from the earth.' So they made this decision that day: 'Let us fight against every man who comes to attack us on the sabbath day; let us not all die as our brethren died in their hiding places'" (2:45, 48). Between the lines of Scripture we sense nothing but approval, nothing but praise for what these followers of Yahweh did. "Mattathias and his friends," the biblical author tells us, "went about and tore down the altars. . . . They rescued the law out of the hands of the Gentiles and kings, and they never let the sinner gain the upper hand" (2: 45, 48).

The valiant old man was soon to die. But he died encouraging his people to continue the fight which he had begun. "Pay back the Gentiles in full," he told them, "and heed what the law commands" (2: 68). He was succeeded by his son Judas (Maccabeus), who "extended the glory of his people. Like a giant he put on his breastplate; he girded on his armor of war and waged battles, protecting the host by his sword. He was like a lion in his deeds, like a lion's cub roaring for prey" (3: 3–4).

Judas dedicated the first period of his reign to organizing his men. He had to train an army for battle, so first he weeded out those who might not be useful on the battlefield. "He said to those who were building houses, or were betrothed, or were planting vineyards, or were fainthearted, that each should return to his home, according to the law" (3: 56). To his warriors he said: "Gird yourselves and be valiant. Be ready early in the morning to fight with these Gentiles who have assembled against us to destroy us and our sanctuary. It is better for us to die in battle than to see the misfortunes of our nation and of the sanctuary. But as his will in heaven may be, so he will do" (3: 58–60).

That day was a day of "great deliverance" for Israel (4: 25). Judas captured the sword of Apollonius (3: 12); he wiped out the army of Seron (3: 23); he slaughtered three thousand men of Gorgias' army (4: 15); he made Lysias retreat to Antioch (4: 34–35); he displayed the head of Nicanor just outside Jerusalem (7: 47). He saved Israel from shame and dishonor.

And when the hour came for him to die, he died as the most valiant of soldiers (9: 1–22). King Demetrius sent a strong army against Jerusalem. Under the command of Bacchides, twenty thousand foot soldiers and two thousand cavalry soldiers set out for Berea. Judas waited for them at Elasa. He had only three thousand men. Of these, many panicked and took flight when they saw the enormous number facing them. Judas was left with eight hundred, and some of these tried to persuade him to retreat. But the intrepid leader ordered an attack. "Judas said, 'Far be it from us to do such a thing as to flee from them. If our time has come, let us die bravely for our brethren, and leave no cause to question our honor.' " He died in that battle. His brothers Jonathan and Simon took his body and buried it in their ancestral tomb, in the city of Modein. And this is how his story ends: "All Israel made great lamentation for him; they mourned many days and said, 'How is the mighty fallen, the savior of Israel!' Now the rest of the acts of Judas, and his wars and the brave deeds that he did, and his greatness, have not been recorded, for they were very many."

A GIANT AMONG DWARFS

Years ago—centuries ago, in fact—a man gave himself up to ordinary work, silently and inconspicuously. For thirty years he lived that way, retaining in his heart the message of peace, and the knowledge of heaven, which he had come to bring to all people. Then he retired to the desert, where the wild beasts protected him from humans. He prayed for forty days, with eyes turned toward God his Father. Then he returned in the direction of his Father's house, and when he saw what was happening there he was astounded. God's house was now a house of business. The temple was a salesroom.

There he found the whited sepulchres, the kind of people who place heavy burdens on the shoulders of others and never lift a finger to help them; who pray out loud in order to be heard by others; who drop coins in the collection basket so that the sound will make them appear generous; who fulfill only the letter of the law; who "keep holy the day of the Lord" only according to the letter.

Eighteen years previously, as a child, he had been in the same temple; he had taught there. Now some of the very people he had taught were still there, but they had grown older, superficial, indifferent.

It is an ordinary market day like any other. The sellers shout the praises of their wares. Children laugh, beasts bellow; the ground is dirty and slippery. People go in and out; the door bangs. Priests and lay people go about their business. Yahweh is praised. Beggars plead for alms. One or two of the leaders remember scenes long past, of that child who explained the Scriptures to them.

Everything is as usual. But suddenly there is a crash—and then silence, deep silence. Then the shouting breaks out again, more vehement this time, much louder; it is a full-scale riot. Money and wares are flung to the floor. Lashes and cracks of a whip! Consternation among the rich, well-fed merchants!

The man with the message of peace and the knowledge of heaven seizes a rope whip. His eyes blaze with fury. He is like a giant among dwarfs. And we ask: Isn't this man the son of the carpenter? Didn't he bless the peace lovers? Isn't he the friend of children? Didn't he promise the earth to the gentle? Where is the Good Shepherd now? Where is his kindness? Where is his mercy?

The penetrating gaze of divine anger in the flesh: such is the face of our young Christ as he enters the house of God, a house transformed into one of hypocrisy. And keep in mind that this is, according to the Gospel of John

(2: 13–22), the very first step in Christ's public life. The hands which will later give health to those who touch them are now lashing out at everyone in their way.

In God's house there is no place for "dogs and sorcerers and fornicators and murderers and idolaters," or for anyone "who loves and practices falsehood" (Rev 22: 14).

"Zeal for thy house has consumed me" (Ps 69: 9; Jn 2: 17). What contrasts we find in the life of God among humans: fierce anger and terrible fury side by side with infinite gentleness and utter tranquility; passionate silences, and cracks of a whip. This is he who will be led like a lamb to the slaughter: the same Lamb of God who will never utter a word as he is led back, on that sad night, from Gethsemane to Jerusalem; who will remain silent in the face of vile insults, blows, and blasphemies, because such silences are the demands of sacrificial love. The same man now knots together lengths of rope to eject everyone from the temple, because those are the demands of another form of love, a consuming zeal for his Father's house.

A whip! Lord, remove from our lives all that falsehood—if necessary, with a whip. What rotten carcasses would then be revealed!

I am well aware that some narrow-minded people will be scandalized by these pages; but that is not going to stop me. Jesus was well aware that the Pharisees were scandalized by some of the things he said, and his answer to that was: "Let them alone; they are blind guides" (Mt 15: 14).

If Christ were to walk into one of our temples today, would he make another whip and use it on the hypocrites? That is a point on which we should each examine our own conscience. I think that rather than inspiring anger, we would inspire only pity in his heart. Of course, he would no longer find oxen or money-tables . . . But have you ever asked yourself what, exactly, Christ does find in you yourself when you pray in his house?

Never let God's house be for you a dark place where you go to hide, from yourself and from others, your fear, your lukewarmness, your worries, your cowardice. Never profane it with pharisaical hypocrisy. Never hide yourself there simply because you are incapable of withstanding the bright light of the sun with that sacred pride and stalwart spirit which properly belong to all good Christians.

God's house should be for you a refuge in time of sorrow—go in, go near the Lord when life has hurt you, when you feel the weight of your own nothingness, when you need strength to bear your weakness and to help you begin all over again with humility and determination. But above all, God's house should be for you a burning furnace where from time to time you renew the red heat of your decisions born of love.

Christians, the Lord is calling us!

The world needs us! Can we meet its needs? Of course we can. "We are able" (Mk 10: 39). Christ and his apostles lead the way!

Forward, soldiers of Christ!

4. You: A Soldier of Christ

YET I WILL LEAVE SEVEN THOUSAND IN ISRAEL, ALL THE KNEES THAT HAVE NOT BOWED TO BAAL.

—1 Kings 19: 18

THESE DAYS

If we do embark on the adventure of life, we will inevitably come up against circumstances and events that are difficult and dangerous—which is only to be expected! But is it not human to defy the beast, to brush aside the decrepit old self that tries to hold us back? Are you going to let your true self be discouraged?

We have come into the world in a moment of grave crisis and misfortune. We hear in our day so many complaints and lamentations, and many of them are justified. But is there any justification for our young people to take a dismal view of today's world?

I say no. Youth is the best time for acquiring sanctity, the ideal time to begin to live an ideal. This is true of all youth of any period in history, but the youth of today have had the good luck—for we believe in luck, which is really Divine Providence—to be born in perhaps the most interesting period in the whole history of humanity. Many of today's young Christians live zealously and energetically; they are happy to be living at such an exciting time as this. The only thing they find frightening is humdrum-ness, or mediocrity Not the humdrumness of everyday routine; for every day brings with it its own challenges. No, they fear only one thing: that cowardly vulgarity which is sin. They hate mediocrity. They hate to do things by halves. They are repelled by the attitude of pessimists, of those people who see only the difficulties of everything. And they are not afraid to live in the world as Christians.

Those young people who are true Christians are very happy to be living in this age, because they see how much there is to be done, and they want to do it. It pains them to see the sadness of people who do not love one another, who invent new forms of martyrdom for one another. They see that the Church is persecuted, and that their brothers and sisters are exhausted. They want to defend them. And they are not thinking in terms of martyrdom. They are young and have no wish to get themselves killed. If they must die in the fight someday, they are determined to die fighting, but they think it is too easy to become a hero in a moment. They wish to feel deeply the heroism of living every day, day after day, for Christ.

Anyone who complains about the age in which they live is not young. Anyone who spends a lot of time thinking of the great days gone by is old. Today's young people must keep fighting and never sit down to rest. Christians love the spirit of youth, which is brave and generous; they are happy to participate in the struggles of their times. They do not daydream about the good old days, nor about a vague peace in the distant future. They use all their energy; all their love, in the living present; and that requires a continuous effort.

People say that we are suffering from youthful enthusiasm, that we are the ones who dream too much while thinking we are living in reality. Right now, they say, we are inspired by great hopes, by values which incite us, which impel us to great audacity and courage. But, they say, time will awake us out of our sleep. Every generation has stretched out its curly head to see the world and sing with the joy of inexperience, but each generation in gray hairs has withdrawn its wrinkled head and shaken it in contempt and mockery.

I do not know, Lord, what young people have done, or tried to do, in other centuries. History has paid more attention to the elderly and their opinions, presumably because they have seen time pass and have gathered from it—it is to be hoped—some wisdom. All I know, Lord, is that you are looking down at us from a wooden cross—that you are alone, between heaven and earth—and that we have ringing in our ears a cry which we can never forget: "Go forth!" (see Mk 16: 15).

This is the great truth: you and I cannot afford to be concerned about possible conflicts or hardships, praise or mockery, contempt or laughter. The night of the world is passing quickly. Day is drawing near. Let us keep in mind these words of our Holy Father: "[For] faithful, valiant people, . . . the hardships of the present time, the sorrows and the maternal tears of [the Church] are neither a stumbling block nor foolishness, but an occasion and a stimulus to show forth—not in words but by actions—the integrity and unselfishness of their purpose, their un-flinching fidelity, and the sublime generosity of their hearts." [1]

This period of world-threatening wars, of political unrest, of tears and blood, is our age. Why should we fear it? This period of transition toward a new age of fire, this period which brings with it such terrible birth pains, is our age. Why not love it? This period of presumption, of restless activity, of loving without knowing what love is, is our age. Why not live it?

Turn your eyes to Christ. Ask him to open them for you. Then you will understand, and become enthusiastic about, the most challenging and rewarding of human adventures, which we will discuss later: the adventures of a generous life, of hard work, of sorrow, of failure, of death.

ONE IDEAL: CHRIST

So far, we have been speaking of lesser human values. Now we come to the great value of your human life. Christ: there you have the great value. There you have the most vigorous and most conscientious of all protests against the present age. Christ: there you have the light. There you have the one name which has been given us above all other names (see Phil 2:9). If we fully realized what we were saying every time our filthy mouths pronounced that name, we would feel a freshness, a serenity, a satisfaction, a thrill so great that a soul can experience none greater. Christ: there you have the end of your restless search for a better and fuller life. Christ: there you have the Absolute which clarifies all our ambitions.

Christians, and all young people, listen to me: we are a race of gods, and only God can satisfy our desires. Do not smile with that smirk of an old cynic; I am telling you the simple truth. Outside of Christ you will never find peace! Never! Outside of Christ cannot be found eternal happiness, which is what we are looking for. Outside of Christ our lives will rot with disease and hatred.

Turn your eyes toward the young Christ, who is *perfectus Deus, perfectus homo,* and you will enter a new life without faltering. Do not be so old and moanful that you think you can do nothing in life that will make any real difference. With Christ beside you, you can feel the pride of making a life-or-death difference on a global scale.

We can change the world, because we are united to Christ and Christ owns the world! "Since we have these promises, beloved, let us cleanse ourselves from every defilement of body and spirit, and make holiness perfect in the fear of God" (2 Cor 7: 1). What more positive precept could you want, as an encouragement to lead a life of Christian ambition?

"We must have great confidence, for it is most important that we should not cramp our good desires, but should believe that, with God's help, if we make continual efforts to do so, we shall attain, though perhaps not at once, to that which many saints have reached through his favor." [2] It is St. Teresa of Avila who says that to us, in her autobiography. And again she insists on this same point. "I am astounded," she says, "at how much can be done on this road if one has the courage to attempt great things; the soul may not have the strength to achieve these things at once, but if it takes a flight it can make good progress." [3]

The Lord our God loves lively souls, vigorous beginnings, strong jolts. God stipulates only one thing in our ambition: that we place all our trust in him. That is the key to success. Promise him that you will shamelessly be a follower of Christ.

AMBITIOUS HORIZONS

LIKE A VINE I CAUSED LOVELINESS TO BUD, AND MY BLOSSOMS BECAME GLORIOUS AND ABUNDANT FRUIT.

— Sirach 24: 17

You were a quiet-living, peaceful person. All your cares and worries were centered on yourself; you never interfered in other people's affairs. Your desires, your ambitions, were confined to a petty and ridiculous little world of your own, but you thought it was immense, because the tentacles of your imagination spread out wide in all directions. When you were alone, when you left the people with whom you were speaking, you always resumed the conversation with yourself. It was a continuous monologue, a fanciful novel in which pride, vanity, passion, had all proclaimed you the central personage of the world, and the shadows applauded your great deeds. You were the leading character, the protagonist, the hero. By keeping up with the lives of the rich and the famous, you added to your imaginative resources the latest success story, the latest adventure. The real world did not yet recognize you, but the moment was coming when it would have to ask your help. You would let them go on asking at the beginning, but finally you would be forced, with a bored gesture, to accept that distinguished position, those public honors, the leadership of the working class, a seat among the powers that be. The way was easy. Much too easy, in fact. Your imagination knew absolutely nothing about responsibility, nothing about hard work, nothing about difficulties, nothing about the cross. You were a quiet-living, peaceful person, too young to know about such things.

Then the spring of your life came into full bloom, and all around you were sounds of war and cries of hunger. You woke up to reality and found yourself being tugged by the arm, by someone other than yourself. You closed your eyes tightly for a moment, then opened them and awoke from that dream which was tormenting you, and you saw in front of you other eyes, which were asking for bread. A child with a pimpled and cretinous face held out an open hand. You wondered why. You understood nothing. You made a gesture of horror and contempt, and when you tried to escape from these ghastly shadows— that is the name you gave to reality—a chorus of hungry laughter pierced your very bones.

Your soul uttered a cry of cowardice and anger. The laughter ceased for a moment, but then became more savage than before: more insulting, more penetrating.

You elbowed your way through the mass of living rottenness. What did you care about the hunger of others? Why did they not spend their time dreaming, like you, instead of running around in the streets? Why did they keep shouting at you, when you so obviously knew and cared nothing about them?

And when you had escaped from those beasts—that is what you called them—you tried to go back to your world of dreams as before; your own little world, so peaceful and quiet.

But now the shadows, the very same shadows as before—the shadows that used to applaud your great deeds, that used to submit to your every wish, that raised you above everybody else—the same ghosts that served you so meekly before, now slinked sorrowfully away and shunned your very presence. You tried to catch them, but they slipped through your fingers. The voices of reality spoke of death and conflict. You felt cold and tired. The shadows no longer satisfied your ambitions. You wanted to dream what you dreamed as a child, but you had forgotten it all, and it refused to come back.

And that fellow human being who tugged you by the arm came again to awaken you, to say to you: "What are you doing? Wake up! What are you doing that has any connection with reality? These people are begging for help. Why do you refuse to help them? These are men, women, and children who have neither health nor a country, nor even a God. They live in utter misery. Their souls are empty of ideals. Do you not want to give them a little relief, a little life, so that they need not continue to crawl along in spiritual decay and rottenness?"

And then you began to wake up! At the beginning, a little afraid and uncertain; later, with a lively enthusiasm.

You recognized that you were in the world for something more than dreaming. You could not go through life wrapped up in your own egotistic shell. You had to do something which would not be self-centered. You, from the moment you opened your eyes to the light of day, by the grace of God, were a Christian. You were, in fact, a soldier of Christ enlisted for a holy campaign. You remembered the words of the catechism, words which you had learned by heart as a child, and now they made you smile. Up to now you had never understood their full significance. And you began to repeat to yourself inwardly, but the words could be read on your lips: "Soldier of Christ! Soldier of Christ? Me, a soldier of Christ?" And you fixed your eyes on the eyes of your friend, and repeated, "Soldier of Christ," without realizing that a great resolution was taking shape in your heart, a resolution formed and fostered by grace. You grasped your friend's hand and shook it violently. "You can count on me," you said. "I will do something for them." And that friend thought, "It's not me that's counting on you; it is the Lord!"

I happened to run into you a few days after you had made your decision. I had no need to ask you anything. You were full of enthusiasm—something mostly human, but also divine. You were like a little boat swept along by the force of the wind. You did not grudge any sacrifice. In fact, you could not understand those self-centered people who were still living as you yourself had been living such a short while before. Why did they not follow your example? Everything seemed small to you. Everything that you did appeared little.

How well you behaved during those days. You walked along at the brisk pace of a triumphal march. The apostolate had become part of you, and an enormous joy took possession of your whole life—contagious joy. It spread to the souls of those who lived near you, and carried them toward God. Up to then you had understood something of love affairs, at least of a few love affairs. Now you began to understand something of Love itself.

WEAKNESS OF THE FLESH

IN YOUR STRUGGLE AGAINST SIN YOU HAVE NOT YET RESISTED TO THE POINT OF SHEDDING YOUR BLOOD.

— Hebrews 12:4

But some time later we meet again. You are completely changed. What has happened to you? Where is that energy, that love which you had, that enthusiasm, that vigor with which you began? You see me in the distance, and you speak to me only with your silence and your downcast eyes. At last you take courage and speak, and you blurt out some ridiculous explanation: "It was only a mistake, a childish mistake. I see now that no matter what I do, the world will go right on in exactly the same way. And besides . . ." You lower your head in shame. "Go on. Tell me the rest." And you, obviously irritated, shout at me, "It's only that . . . being chaste is too hard! I can't do it!"

Well, in reply to such nonsensical reasons, such silly arguments, all I can say is, you coward! Your eyes blaze and you stare at me, but I am not afraid to say it again. You coward! You "can't"—what you mean is, you don't want to! With people like you, Christianity would have died out long before the time of the catacombs. Others are content to do very little, you say? For that very reason you should be determined to do more. The scarecrow of discouragement frightens you. Then you get up—not to walk away, but to run away. But I have the last word. I am telling you right now: there are duties which must not be avoided, regardless of how downhearted or discouraged you may be.

Though much of what I am about to say applies just as well to women, I would like to direct it specifically to you men. Certainly, especially in today's world, it takes great courage and strength of character for anyone of either gender to live a chaste life. But men do have an extra problem: namely, a widespread prejudice that chastity is something unmanly, that chastity and real manhood are mutually exclusive categories. This mistaken notion is very harmful to both men and women.

Like St. John, therefore, I want now to "write to you, young men, because you are strong, and the word of God abides in you, and you have overcome the evil one" (1 Jn 2: 14). And keep this in mind: I do realize that you and I and all of us men are made of clay and are always capable of sinning. Nevertheless . . .

Right now—this very moment—is the time for Christian men to prove to the world, in very practical and concrete ways, that any normal man can live perfect and absolute chastity, provided that he avoids occasions of sin and prays for grace. St. Josemaría sounds the rallying cry: "There is need for a crusade of manliness and purity to counteract and nullify the savage work of those who think man is a beast. And that crusade is *your* work." [4]

Young man: Head held high, a generous soul, a clean body! Manliness! Yes, you say, but what about guys with mental or emotional problems? Can they live chastely? Can their young adulthood be pure and healthy? Well, I am not speaking here of people who are psychotic or otherwise deranged. I'm not talking about guys who literally have no self-control and who therefore need to be institutionalized. I am speaking of normal men, perfectly healthy or not so healthy, who have all the emotions, inclinations, and impulses that other men have, but who labor, who struggle, who fight to overcome every temptation, however strong.

Temptations, struggles, sneers, danger, death: that's all part of life! But is a soldier frightened by the sounds of battle? War is always accompanied by the rattle of arms.

Never let me hear you say "I can't." We have sufficient grace always to come out smiling from any trial, however violent. But, of course, we must never enter into danger voluntarily. That would be tempting God. For those of us who love the dangers of the new and the unknown, a soldier of Christ has said: "Don't be such a coward as to be 'brave.' Flee!" [5] Listen to the Apostle: "In your struggle against sin you have not yet resisted to the point of shedding your blood" (Heb 12:4). Does that frighten you? You thought, perhaps, that to shun occasions of sin would be a simple thing? When the flesh rebels against the spirit, when the concept of hell no longer frightens you, when miserable arguments keep tormenting you, then do whatever it takes to gain mastery over the flesh, "lest my enemy say, 'I have prevailed over him'; lest my foes rejoice because I am shaken" (Ps 13:4). As St. Josemaría suggests in *The Way* (no. 214), "Say to your body: 'I would rather keep you in slavery than be myself your slave.'"

There is no middle course. Animal or saint: choose!

Virility! Manliness! You think there are some saints who had no temptations? Wrong. It's simply that with the help of God their Father, they never neglected the human means, and at times they rose to superhuman heights to gain a supernatural victory. Psalm 66 (verse 12) tells us that before we rest, we must go through fire and water. The books say so little of how the saints had to fight. Yet how they did have to fight! And with what willpower!

I repeat, I am speaking of normal men. We leave the abnormal in the hands of their doctors, to be examined and treated as pathological cases. Those incapable of self-control, those proud to be perverted or promiscuous—such men should not read these pages. They will never understand what manliness is. And so many of them think they are more manly than other men! But they lack willpower, which is human strength. More manly? Actually, they are more like animals. What a degenerate race! Contagious diseases cannot deter them, they are so consumed by passion.

So much for my aside to the men. Returning once more to all of my readers, I remind you that much of what I have stated here applies equally to women. All Christians need to realize that to give in to one's every urge is not—contrary to popular opinion—"only human." It is subhuman—not human at all.

People have, consciously and deliberately, invented religions that are very easy to adhere to: religions which allow them to do whatever they like. In contrast, our religion, which is God's religion, makes demands on us. To see this as something negative is a terrible mistake, and a common one—specially with regard to the sixth commandment. It is very sad that so many of us regard it as an obstruction to our happiness.

We have a lot to learn, a lot to rethink. We have been brought up to look at the problem from a wrong angle. Is there, in God's law, only one real commandment—the sixth? Often that is the only one that people think of. Well, very much has been written about this commandment, and for good reason: it has to do with matters of vital concern to nearly everyone. But often it is treated in such a sorrowful way, in a tone so strong—implying that its purpose is oppression—that young readers are inevitably drawn toward the very evil they are being warned against.

One comes across statements like this: "Those who

wish to give all their love to any great enterprise must subject themselves to chastity." That is not true! Chastity is not subjection; it is liberation. Chastity is not for the wimpy—nobody is born chaste—but for the strong, for the healthy. Strong, healthy people, when they feel the same urges which lead others to illicit pleasure, sacrifice all that for the love of God, of that God who alone holds the secret of satisfying all the desires, all the longings, all the ambitions of the poor human heart. You know well how to remedy your situation, and yet you still speak of it as being a problem of purity. Yours is not a problem of purity; it is a problem of laziness. Possibly physical and mental laziness, as well, but definitely spiritual laziness.

Continue with that out-of-focus, useless life of yours. Let your go-with-the-flow feelings overcome you as usual at the time for getting up. Go to bed at any old time, whenever you happen to feel like it. Make no effort to form a plan of life. Waste time as usual. Spend as much time as you can in idle pursuits. Let your eyes rest on anything they notice, let your imagination wander freely, and, lazy coward that you are, you will soon see how wide are the gates of hell.

The problem of purity is simply a problem of substitution. As long as you have no passion stronger than that of the flesh, you will continue to fall and wallow in the filthy mud again and again, and in that way you will become blind to the light of heaven. You will become insensitive to the life of the spirit. Yes, it is a problem of substitution. Do not think that you will control the flesh through fear of hell, or fear of death; in times of temptation, these ideas have no meaning. And do not think that you will remedy your inclinations by determination alone. Willpower is very important, but by itself it is very little.

We will speak later of the remedy for this weakness. And in the meantime, take to heart this advice from St. Josemaría: "Never despair. Lazarus was dead and decaying: . . . 'by now he will smell; this is the fourth day,' Martha told Jesus. If you hear the inspiration of God and follow it— . . . 'Lazarus, come forth!'—you will return to Life." [6]

WEAKNESS OF SOUL

YOU'RE BORED? THAT'S BECAUSE YOU KEEP YOUR SENSES AWAKE AND YOUR SOUL ASLEEP.

    — St. Josemaría Escrivà, *The Way*, no. 368

Now you tell me it is no longer the weakness of the flesh that discourages you, it is the weakness of your interior life. It is, you say, a weakness that paralyzes all your efforts; you get very tired. And finally you confess that you are bored by everything having to do with God.

This is cause indeed for grave concern. For even mortal sin, which makes the soul a filthy skeleton bereft of grace, is less dangerous than that despondency, that discouragement, which takes away all the joy that we should be getting from continually starting out anew in our spiritual life. For sons and daughters of God, for souls who habitually live in the state of grace, sin is a false step, a mistake, a fall which prompts them to rise again at once and continue on the road to sanctity. Discouragement, on the other hand, is a powerful enemy which paralyzes all life.

It is characteristic of people who are old in spirit, of those who "have seen it all," that they never see a remedy for their own condition or for that of the world. They are weak and flabby of temperament and need a hand of iron to push them ahead in life. Perhaps they started out full of energy, but one fall, then another, and another, extinguished the light which showed them the way. They have remembered nothing but their negative experiences: their disappointments, downfalls, failures, temptations, downheartedness. Everything seems impossible to them. They lack the Christian outlook on life: faith and sacrifice. And so, every heroic deed becomes for them impossible.

This shadow of despondency often makes its way into the interior life when a soul, having at first been carried away by sentimental consolation and exalted emotions, begins to see that the flame of devout feelings is dying out. Interior progress is impeded by false concepts and faulty logic. The sweetness with which the presence of God may be accompanied at the beginning—little favors which God gives to whom he wishes, because he so wishes, and which are no indication of the actual progress of a soul—should develop into a "voluntary" presence of God, an awareness stemming from the will and not from the feelings. One needs to make deliberate efforts and devise little tactics to keep Christ before one's eyes. And that is something many people cannot do, because they lack proper formation.

You must learn to detest the falsehood of all sentimental acts of devotion that are not grounded in the will. Otherwise you will advance very slowly in your Christian life—a life which should be robust; a life which should go ahead at a brisk pace. Remember that in spiritual life, as in physical life, there can be no stagnation. Either you go forward or you go backward. Love allows no standing still.

It is not that you are tired! Your soul is despondent simply because you bring to your interior life the same frivolity which frustrates all your human actions. Do not act on the surface. Get to the bottom of things—go deep into your soul with prayer and sacrifice—and forget these sentimentalities.

Peter and his companions have stayed up all night working hard, trying to catch some fish in the waters of Gennesaret (see Lk 5: 1–5). They have caught nothing. But as soon as they set foot on land—before tiredness and sleepiness can overcome them—they begin to wash and repair their empty nets in preparation for the following night's fishing. This is the way with men and women of hope. With all their energy they row against the current, praising God when the skies are favorable and never losing heart when the waves rise against them.

How sad it is to see those souls, those generous souls, who are thirsty and are longing for the heights, but who lose heart easily, who give up, whose courage fails them. In those hearts there is lacking a divine value which is absolutely necessary for all human actions: a life of faith; a life of faith and sacrifice. If we lose faith, in what can we hope?

Live the virtue of courage, which is the driving force of all acts of the spirit, and you will cure your spiritual anemia. Trusting in the goodness of God, cast out from your soul that shadow, that phantom, which is frightening you and holding you back, that sly worm which undermines all your energy, that pessimistic despondency which makes you lead the life of a mediocre animal. It whispers in your ear continually: "You can't. That is not for you. What is all this talk of sanctity and heroism, of ambition and struggles?"

Be courageous in your reaction. Look at Christ. Listen to that response of John and James: "We are able" (Mk 10: 39). And for the first time you will feel another virtue spring up in your maturity: youthfulness.

DESERTION

DO YOUR BEST TO COME TO ME SOON. FOR DEMAS . . .
HAS DESERTED ME.

— 2 Timothy 4: 9

Consider the sorrow of the last apostle of Christ, on seeing himself abandoned by an old friend he has thought unshakable.

Paul is now old. His loyalty to God has brought him into a new field of action. And Demas, a friend who has accompanied him in many of his travels, is frightened. He knows what prison is like and has no wish to find himself there again. After an interior struggle which he cannot avoid, he retires to the easy life of his home, to the peace and quiet of his own family; he deserts Paul and flees to Thessalonica. Meanwhile, Crescens and Titus, also friends of the old apostle and, like Paul himself, servants of Christ, have had to go to Galatia and Dalmatia, respectively. Paul is left almost alone.

In his second letter to Timothy we read of his grief. "Do your best," he urges Timothy, "to come to me soon. For Demas, in love with this present world, has deserted me and gone to Thessalonica. . . . Luke alone is with me." He is already beginning to feel the cold of death. "When you come," he says, "bring the cloak that I left with Carpus at Troas, also the books, and above all the parchments."

What a contrast: loyalty and treachery! The faithfulness of Paul and the desertion of one of his spiritual children! Desertion! Betrayal! Demas, Judas, Pilate, the young man who went sadly away from the presence of our Lord . . . Judas turns traitor out of despair; Pilate, out of willingness to compromise; the unnamed young man, out of love of money; and now Demas, out of love of comfort. They are all betrayers of Christ. What little loyalty they all showed.

When I see you stop or hesitate along the way you once courageously chose, I feel like giving you a good swift kick, to wake you up before treachery gets a foothold in your soul. Try to realize that you must keep on crying, *"Serviam!* I will serve! I will be faithful to you unto death!" Do you not see that you must, as St. Josemaría insists, continue to be faithful "even at the cost of fortune, of honor, and of life"? [7] Simply because things become difficult for you—because you are threatened by prison, or unruly desires of the flesh, or depression, or pride—are you going to give up being loyal to God? At the first difficulty are you going to throw down the cross which you were carrying for him who called you? Do you not hear the voice of Christ, the sigh of God, whispering in your ear: "Friend, why are you here?" (Mt 26: 50).

You were furious—I saw you—a few years ago when your country's flag was soiled in the clotted blood of a hundred filthy crimes. I saw your anger! The honor of your homeland was being violated, and you hurried to the trenches, forgetting your loved ones and your own life, to defend it. Today, all that seems so far away and so insignificant.

Your soul was searching for something; your heart was not content with the shattered remains of days gone by; and in your path you met a special someone. That meeting dazzled your heart with pictures of a home. "What happy days," you are thinking now, as you remember them. But that generous love died when, for some reason or other, time separated you from your sweetheart.

You had some other ambitions. You went to the university with great illusions. A few years went by, and with them all your ambitions. "I must work with great energy in spite of everything," you said to yourself. But your ideals quietly faded away. You read some books about famous people of bygone days, and for a while vanity made your days pass by more quickly. But every one of those books ended with the death of the protagonist. Your restless eyes stared pensively at the leafy trees.

That was not the life which your imagination had thought up. The nurturing of your children, the happiness in your poor and humble family, your professional work—it all broke up, bit by bit, like dry mud in your hands. And now you are calm. Too calm; with the quietness of the grave.

"I know your works, your toil and your patient endurance, and how you cannot bear evil men. . . . I know you are enduring patiently and bearing up for my name's sake, and you have not grown weary. But I have this against you, that you have abandoned the love you had at first" (Rev 2: 2–4).

I will tell you the reason for these failures, and you will find a reason for living, and an adventure in each day. Because the days are not all equally colorless and monotonous. Let me tell you the reason for all that weakness in your flesh, in your soul, in your youthfulness.

Even when you thought you were aspiring to great things, your ambition was petty, your desires never went far, and your emotions were never very deep. Time was bound to wipe them all out, completely. If you want to do something, or be something, in life, you must give your spirit a much higher ideal, an indestructible hope, an infinite desire, an almost unattainable target. You were disillusioned when you realized that, even if you were to attain the object you desired, it would still be petty and incapable of filling your young life.

For you the earth now seemed small. You wished to be happy, and the failure that you met in your search for greatness and beauty made you drift into narrow waters and limit your desires. That would be better, you thought. You did not have the courage to admit your defeat.

I will tell you the reason for your failure. You stood on the hills and looked at the mountains—at the empty and motionless earth. You should have looked much higher. You should have had a limitless perspective—above the clouds; above the sun. You should have looked at Christ!

You must contemplate Christ, and study him seriously, and let yourself be saturated with him, and let yourself be carried away, and become crazy for that great ideal. In that way your youth will be something, it will be much, it will be everything.

And then your generous love will return; you will look at that same special someone and fall in love for good. And then the trenches will have a meaning for you again. And then people's lives will no longer remind you of death. And then your children's nurturing will be assured. And when night comes, you will smile, although tired by the day's work. And the sorrows of your loved ones will be changed to joy; and your profession, your work, will become a road, a way, which will take you far ahead. And you will gain mastery of the appetites of the flesh, and the things of God will attract you enormously. And nothing will break in your hands. And you will conquer; you will find the victorious solution to that deep insecurity, that ulcerous doubt, which now tortures your heart.

SINCERITY AND CONSTANCY

BE FAITHFUL UNTO DEATH, AND I WILL GIVE YOU THE CROWN OF LIFE.

— Revelation 2: 10

Speak out! Do not hide that dangerous situation in which you find yourself. Break those fetters of tormenting silence which keep you in subjection. Pour out your heart to someone who knows your soul. Tell that person the treacherous plans you are contemplating. Be sincere, even if in these moments of intense pain it is agonizing for you to speak. I assure you, as a priest of God, that I do not know of one single person who has strayed from the true path when he had the courage and the sincerity to open up the hidden corners of his soul. And as a priest of God I also assure you that I do know souls who out of cowardice and dishonesty have lost the greatest treasure which can be had on this earth.

"Friend, why are you here?" To put up a front, or to sanctify yourself? It is not yet too late. Afterward it may be. Soon it will be. Do not be ashamed. There is much remodeling to be done, but think of the joy and the peace which sincerity brings with it. You're wondering, what will people say? They will say that you have been courageous. You will gain esteem and admiration. And from that moment on, you will have the help, the empathy, the moral support, as well as the prayer and the sacrifice, of that person entrusted with the care of your soul, that person who might even be willing to die for you rather than let you turn your back on God.

"Look," St. Josemaría reminds you, "the apostles, for all their evident and undeniable weaknesses, were sincere, simple . . . transparent. You, too, have evident and undeniable weaknesses. May you not lack simplicity." [8]

If you have not done so already, go to confession. Now, after that sacramental confession, your soul is free of the dead weight it has been carrying for so long. Sincerity has cost you a terrible effort of humility, but it is a voluntary humility which will be an expiation for all your miseries. Now you are free. Once again God is in your soul. You are that prodigal son, that completely loved and forgiven child, whom Jesus was talking about.

Now you must prove your sincerity with good works. Otherwise, do not ask me to believe in your repentance. Let me tell you again: Love is deeds, not words.

How often have you begun, fallen back, and begun again to climb the paths of your soul which lead to God?

Many times I have found you downhearted. You have told me that you cannot go on, and you have said it with tears in your eyes. You have said that the flesh will not allow you to have a supernatural outlook on what goes on around you; that your passionate temperament causes you to look at life optimistically at one moment, only to be flung at the very next moment into the tortures and agonies of depression. Exaltation and pessimism follow one another in quick succession. You become enthusiastic often, and just as often you lose heart. You are full of life, and then you relapse into numbness. You are well acquainted both with the Eucharist and with sin, with prayer and with disregard for God, with the spirit that is willing and with the flesh that is weak. You say that when things go badly, you can never carry out the resolutions you made when things were going well. Then you look at me with obvious frustration and anger and finally get up the courage to say: "Leave me alone. Mind your own business. Just leave me in peace. When I stop thinking about God, at least I have some peace."

But I cannot leave you, because you have been called to do great things and, instead, you are committing spiritual suicide. I cannot leave you alone. We will travel the road together. You need never despair. Look at Peter, denying his Master because he is afraid of a servant-girl. But Peter then weeps over his sin, and that is why we find in him the rock on which the Church is founded.

Look at Thomas, who refuses to believe in the resurrection of Christ until he can touch the wounds with his own hands; until he can satisfy himself as to the holes made by the nails. But an outburst of faith remedies all his faults, as Peter's tears have remedied his.

And, before all that, look at all of these specially chosen men who have spent so much time at the side of Jesus. They believe that he is the Son of God. They have seen breathtaking miracles performed quite easily by the hands of their Master. They have often heard him speak of humility and of the bonds of love which should unite them. And still they have to hang their heads in shame when the Lord asks them what they have been "discussing on the way" (see Mk 9: 33), for they know that he knows. Just imagine, they have been discussing at the top of their voices which of them will be the greatest in the kingdom of heaven. But now look at them as they leave the upper room on the morning of Pentecost. They have been transformed.

If you place yourself in the hands of the Holy Spirit, if you abandon yourself to him, your hatred will turn to love, your inconsistency will turn into a steady rock of the Church, your laziness will change to boundless enthusiasm, and your base passions will be vital energy. Do not be afraid of your defects. Listen to the cry of the Apostle: "I will all the more gladly boast of my weaknesses, that the power of Christ may rest upon me" (2 Cor 12: 9). Fight on! Be constant in the struggle! Persevere, in spite of all pain!

Listen to what an atheist philosopher has to say: "To those human beings who are of any concern to me I wish suffering, desolation, sickness, ill-treatment, indignities—I wish that they should not remain unfamiliar with profound self-contempt, the torture of self-mistrust, the wretchedness of the vanquished: I have no pity for them, because I wish them the only thing that can prove today whether one is worth anything or not—that one endures." [9]

Without constancy you will never be any kind of real human being, let alone a saint.

Don't you want to change that great defect of yours, frivolity, into a great virtue? To do so, you must strengthen your will. And you do that by making an effort every day. Do not deceive yourself. You will never learn courage or constancy by reading books on the formation of character. Your own experience tells you that you need a plan of life. And I tell you that you need to stick to it rigidly and never lose sight of it. Stop being a weakling.

What is wrong with you is not tepidity. In order to be tepid, or lukewarm, one must have already lived a true interior life at some previous time. Tepidity is a descent from heights to depths. Your trouble is that you have not yet risen to any heights. That is the cause of your indifference and your wavering.

Make an effort! Get on your feet and follow closely the footsteps of God.

Do not be content to stay between two streams, in a no-man's-land, hesitating, afraid to be a mature person. That type of conduct is contemptible. Make a decision and stick with it.

Do not tell me that you cannot do it. Do you think our God wants wishy-washy or comfort-loving people in his service? In every army there is a rule which prescribes that when you are commanded to stick to your post at all costs, you will do it. The army of Christ is no exception.

Listen once more to St. Josemaría: "Perseverance that nothing can shake. You lack it. Ask it of our Lord and do what you can to obtain it; for perseverance is a great safeguard against your ever turning from the fruitful way you have chosen." [10]

The struggle against yourself is something that will end only when your bones mingle with the cold earth. But do you think it is not worthwhile to put up this struggle for Christ? Your life will be a full one if you do what you ought to do, and be where you ought to be. Begin again every day, begin anew—without being discouraged, without being afraid—constantly.

I tell you, it would be easy to find thousands of people who would march to Rome tomorrow if they were asked to fight in defense of Peter. But it is very difficult to find one friend of God who is willing to put into daily practice—*hodie, nunc*, today, this very moment—that resolution in concrete terms.

You want to be constant, to be firm? Increase your desire for God. He will make of you, of me, of every one of us, an immovable wall of bronze.

Listen to the cry of St. Teresa:

> It is most important—all-important, indeed—that [all those in pursuit of sanctity] should begin well by making an earnest and most determined resolve not to halt until they reach their goal, whatever may come, whatever may happen to them, however hard they may have to labor, whoever may complain of them, whether they reach their goal or die on the road or have no heart to confront the trials which they meet, whether the very world dissolves before them.[11]

5. Into the Deep

"Put out into the deep."

— Luke 5:4

Generosity

My money!" "My land!" "My property!" In the great world of the rich, how often we hear talk of what is "mine" versus "yours."

"My crumbs!" "My rags!" "My misery!" In the immense world of the needy, how often we hear that same distinction of "mine" versus "yours."

"My books!" "My love affairs!" "My family!" In the great field of middle-class workers, how they speak of what is "mine" versus "yours."

In the misers' mansions, in the enterprises of the ambitious, and almost everywhere else, people are using this possessive language: "mine," "yours," and so forth. It is no longer a good idea to say that we should love one another "as brothers and sisters"; at best we should say "as friends," since brothers and sisters so often hate one another and do nothing but bicker, out of selfishness.

The rich, even while helping the poor, despise them, while the poor think that begging is beneath their dignity. If the rich give anything, they throw it as if to a dog. In their eyes there is a look of compassion, but it is false. From their hands the money falls—drenched in blood. They encourage the sick to become resigned, and in their hearts they despise them. Everyone seeks his own advantage, his own glory, and gives only what he does not wish to keep. Everyone makes deep calculations and considers at length before saying, "Take it." Everyone wants to have a friend, but nobody wants to be one. We are all slaves of stinginess; everything we touch is contaminated by the language of "mine" and "yours."

And we have brought this poisonous attitude of mind even into our supernatural life. We give sparingly to other people, and just as sparingly we give to God. In the eyes of us misers, God is no more than a great power to whom one goes to get favors: tolerable health, a bit of money, some consolation in a time of trouble. And, so, our churches are filled with tears and troubles, with petitions and laments. God is approached not as a friend, but only as a benefactor.

It seems, in fact, as if we have decided to be always unhappy with our God. When we are suffering, we toddle along to the church. When we are happy, we enjoy ourselves in a sullen silence and turn our backs on the Lord—our *Lord*, who loves nothing better than our smiles!

Nowadays we are so selfish that we think "generosity" means simply giving alms.

In *The Way* (no. 467) we find a different focus:

> "Books"—I put my hand out, like one of Christ's beggars, and I asked for books—books that are nourishment for the Roman, Catholic, and apostolic minds of many university students. I put my hand out, like one of Christ's beggars, and each time had it brushed aside! Why can't people understand, Jesus, the profound Christian charity of this alms, more effective than a gift of the finest bread?

Today, Christians, as much as non-Christians, are always looking to receive; they seldom if ever experience the joy of giving. That is why they do not know what love is. They do not understand that to love means to give oneself. With today's Christians you have to use the same tactics as with little children—to make them take their medicine, you must promise them something. To get them to give alms, you have to offer them charity concerts, fundraising dinners, raffles, candy bars. They will not take part in study circles or apostolic activities unless they are offered coffee and pastries at break-time.

We have to be tricked into fulfilling our duties as Christians! Something has clearly gone wrong. Actually, though, anyone who comes to Christianity for selfish gain should go away. What they will find in Christianity is a heavy cross made for criminals, and on it a suffering God holding out torn hands—hands that are open and making an appeal.

Into these hands, the hands of our God, we who are Christians can pour money, books, our intelligence, our work, our ambitions. The blood-stained face of our crucified God is still appealing to us. It is asking for our hearts.

And that is, as Giovanni Papini points out, a request that few today are willing to heed: "You offer to your gods," he tells us bluntly, "that which costs you the least—genuflections, the pronouncing of words, sacrifices both bloody and bloodless, incense and singing— but rarely do you know how to offer either your spirit or your life. Your heart does not belong to eternity; it is enslaved by the belly, by sex, by consuming greed, and by murder." [1]

We characterize as "generous" anyone who gives away a few paltry coins. How miserly we are toward our God!

The world pities Christians who decide to put themselves completely at the service of the Lord. And it pities them precisely because it is itself so utterly greedy, so absolutely selfish, that it is incapable of understanding the motivation behind those decisions.

We must always object to this kind of pity. We cannot allow the self-centered misers of this world to go on thinking that only some disillusionment, some disappointment, can make a person walk a path of total dedication to God.

I must tell you this: it is not those whom the world despises who hold out their hands to God. It is not those whom fate has robbed of their riches who seek shelter in voluntary poverty; not those who have no personality who bind themselves to obey promptly, conscientiously, and lovingly; not the sexless, the frigid, the impotent, or those afraid of marriage who give up the pleasures of the flesh in their pursuit of the pleasures of the spirit.

It is not true that religious life or any other state of total dedication to God is nothing more than a place of refuge for the weak and the timorous. On the contrary, it is precisely the strongest individuals—the most generous, the most courageous, the least selfish—who give their lives to the perpetual service of an ideal, of the most noble of all ideals.

I have written all this especially for those anxious parents who are so worried about the possible self-surrender of their young-adult children that they are making every effort to stop them from offering their lives and their youth. I would urge them to keep in mind this advice from St. Francis de Sales:

> For what are all these things which we despise and abandon for God? Nothing but little worthless moments of liberty, a thousand times more slavish than slavery itself; perpetual disquietudes, and vain, inconstant, and insatiable pretensions, which agitate our souls with a thousand useless solicitudes and

entreaties, and all for these miserable days of life, so uncertain, so short, and so evil.

Nevertheless, so it has pleased God, that he who quits these empty nothings, these vain amusements, [will gain] in exchange for them an eternal and glorious felicity. . . . This single consideration of having resolved to love God with all our heart, and of having gained a single little additional degree of eternal love, will plunge us into an abyss of happiness.[2]

You fathers and mothers of families should be very careful not to do anything which might disturb that holy idea of your children who are thinking of dedicating themselves to God. Do you not see that he needs them? That he has chosen to need them? How is it possible that Christian parents should be afraid to encourage their children to go closer to God in this way? They do not see the harmfulness of what they are doing when they try to dissuade a young person from making a full self-offering to the supreme Lord of the earth. It is very sad to see souls who truly, with mature deliberation and judgment, desire to give up everything forever but are prevented from taking the plunge solely on account of the "prudent" advice of someone who is "only saying it for your own good." You are not necessarily frightened when your daughter gives herself to a man, but you take fright so easily when you discover that she wishes to dedicate herself explicitly and directly to God. And yet you consider yourself Christian!

"She's my child, my child!" I hear your cries. But the reply is quite simple: She is not yours, she is God's!

At times this advice goes further: "Look, son, if they start talking to you about self-surrender and generosity, don't pay any attention to them." Don't you realize that when you say something like this, you are trying to tie God's hands?

You who have children, do not destroy the greatest offering that you can make to God: your children. An only son, or an only daughter, is not excluded from this warning given by our Lord himself: *anyone* who "loves father or mother more than me is not worthy of me"; likewise, anyone who "loves son or daughter more than me is not worthy of me" (Mt 10: 37). Nor is anyone categorically excluded from this invitation of his: *whoever* "has left houses or brothers or sisters or father or mother or children or lands, for my name's sake, will receive a hundredfold, and inherit eternal life" (Mt 19: 29).

You parents who are generous, who are willing to surrender your children, part of your own heart, you will receive a hundredfold reward, including a share in the glory of all the sacred work which they do in the world.

All that I have said so far refers to parents. But there are other cases, less understandable, more deplorable still. How is it possible that individuals who once gave themselves completely should fear that others will give themselves now? They think, perhaps, that the surrender will be inordinately hard for, or cruel to, these young people and their families. And so they never encourage, they only stall or more actively impede the good impulses of those who ask their advice. They cannot have lived their own generosity cheerfully, if they now lack the will to encourage others.

What a disgrace they are! They never want to hear anyone talk of sanctity. It upsets them. They too dreamed of that, years ago, but the struggle eventually exhausted them. They never want to hear of people who are in love with God, because they too were once guilty of the same folly, they too once opened their hearts to all the petitions of their Christ, but today their hearts are full of cracks and crevices which let in the dirty waters of every gutter.

They never want to hear of self-surrender, because their own years-old selfishness, their complete lack of a spirit of sacrifice, urges them on to a feverish search for comforts and compensations to fill the empty hollows of their souls. They never want to hear of generosity, because they themselves deny God everything.

St. John of the Cross severely reprimands those who operate out of this frame of mind:

> Such directors show a wrong spirit, and are undevout, and clad, as it were, in very worldly garb, having little of the tenderness of Christ, since they neither enter themselves, nor allow others to enter. And our Savior says: "Woe unto you that have taken away the key of knowledge, and enter not in yourselves nor allow others to enter!" For these persons in truth are placed like barriers and obstacles at the gate of heaven, remembering not that God has placed them there that they may compel those whom God calls to enter in, as he has commanded; whereas they, on the other hand, are compelling souls not to enter in by the narrow gate that leads to life; in this way such a man is a blind guide who can obstruct the guidance of the Holy Spirit in the soul.[3]

After this outcry from St. John of the Cross, we are left with only a feeling of pity in our hearts for those who, though officially dedicated to God, oppose, delay, or otherwise obstruct the full self-surrender of other souls. What has happened to those individuals, that they should have given up making efforts to receive the hundredfold reward? How can it be that they do not relish their life of service to the glory of the Lord and consequently desire that others should also experience that happiness?

Believe me, we will soon have to set alight in the world a great fire to burn out the selfishness of these token-charity times. And into those flames which would reach right up to heaven, all of us Christians—every last one of us—should throw ourselves, in order to purify ourselves and begin life again seriously.

MORE GENEROSITY

PRUDENCE IS UNDOUBTEDLY A VIRTUE, BUT IT IS NEITHER A VIRTUE NOR EVEN CHRISTIAN IF THE CHRISTIAN MAKES OF IT A COMFORTABLE MASK FOR HIS TEPIDITY AND SELFISHNESS. CAUTIOUS CHRISTIANS ARE UNDOUBTEDLY CAUTIOUS, BUT THEY ARE NOT CHRISTIANS.

— Michele Sciacca, *The Church and Modern Civilization*

It is most unfortunate that we ever learned that phrase *In medio virtus* (Virtue lies in moderation). Especially since we learned it so badly! We learned the motto, but we never bothered to learn what it meant; we were afraid to go into it deeply.

Contrary to popular belief, the theologians, when they speak of the "golden mean" in which virtue is to be found, are not in any way advocating a mediocre way of life. The true interpretation is this: The golden mean is the most desirable point between two undesirable extremes; courage, for example, is that most desirable point between cowardice and recklessness. But our own laziness and love of comfort have given us a second interpretation of the golden mean: a mediocre or "moderate" point between two *virtues*; a point which we apply as we like and which solves all our problems for us.

We have chosen one virtue out of them all, actually a pseudo-virtue that we have falsely called "prudence": an easygoing virtue which urges us on all occasions to stop halfway. There are circumstances which demand a clearly defined attitude, where no beating around the bush is allowed: a yes or a no, nothing in between. And right now every Catholic, every Christian, must adopt one clear and conscious attitude in the fight which is drawing near—a fight which promises to be a gigantic one—because either we undertake the adventure of doing something serious in this life, something in accordance with our ideal, in which case we will have to exert every human faculty we possess, or else we will have to give up calling ourselves Christian. In the struggles of the spirit there can be no neutral parties or conscientious objectors, and no escape. Everyone will act in one way or the other. Only corpses can remain in a no-man's-land.

But the so-called virtuous people of this age tell us: "Be prudent, very prudent. Do not waste your life. Self-surrender? Fine and good, but only in moderation. Extremes of any sort can be dangerous. Prudence!"

Do not listen to them. The theological virtues allow no holding back. Pay no attention to that cowardly advice which comes not from theologians but from cheats.

Can we believe *too much* in God?

Can we hope *too much* in our Father?

Can we love Jesus *too much*?

Let us not allow ourselves to be deceived. Let us believe in the incredible. Let us hope in the impossible. Let us love extravagantly. Let us give over our reason to the folly of the cross. Let us heed the warning of the Holy Spirit concerning those "prudent" deceivers: "And if one asks him, 'What are these wounds on your back?' he will say, 'The wounds I received in the house of my friends'" (Zech 13:6).

Open your eyes and you will fall in love with your loving God. Look: the cross! Now open your ears and listen to the theologians of the Truth: a single drop of that Lover's blood would have sufficed; the slightest humiliation that Christ endured, or a mere desire coming from his heart, would have been sufficient for the complete redemption of humanity.

We open our eyes much wider to look closely at him. Spits, and the whip, and a crown of briars: no pain could be like his pain. And the human beasts fight for his flesh: flesh that smells with a sickening stench. A nail, and a second nail: the whole body writhes. His humanity is beaten and torn; his sobs break out, and he cries to his Father; a criminal blasphemes in his ears; a chorus of laughs, jeers, curses.

Keeping in mind that a single drop of blood, or a mere wish, would have been sufficient, we recall scenes of the previous night, of Jesus surrounded by the hatred of his accusers, and the howling mobs around him cause our eyes to blaze with anger.

We go back a little further and recall the Eucharistic discourse related in the sixth chapter of St. John, in which the Lord asks people for a serious commitment of faith. From that moment on, many of his disciples abandon him. "Will you also go away?" he asks his friends, the Twelve. Judas is there; he is one of the eleven who say nothing in response, but the only one whose silence Jesus recognizes as a vote of no confidence.

Judas will speak out on that most sorrowful night, that night when our Lord is deserted by those who up to then have called themselves his. In the olive orchard his closest friends fall asleep. Their eyes are heavy with slumber, while Christ sweats drops of blood. But the traitor is awake. In the hearts of the other apostles there is no fire—the only fire in that darkness is that of the torches of hate carried by those who come to capture Jesus. Judas, "one of the Twelve" (Mt 26: 47), kisses him, while the others run away. On that occasion when he asked for a serious commitment of faith, very many abandoned him. Now, when serious sacrifice may be involved, no one remains. The young man wearing the linen cloth—the last friend mentioned in the Gospel of Mark (14: 51)—will also desert him. For a long time he is utterly alone, surrounded by nothing but hatred and fury; the very few loved ones who never actually desert him (his mother, for example) are unable to remain physically near him throughout his ordeal.

The noise increases. The leaders of the people begin to accuse him. Pilate can find no fault in this man, but that makes no difference to them. With one voice, all the people cry out: "Away with this man, and release to us Barabbas!" (Lk 23: 18). Pilate is still in favor of releasing Jesus, but they cry out: "Crucify him!" He makes an effort and says, "Why, what evil has he done?" But they insist again and again, with loud cries, that he should be crucified. And the shouting increases.

"Why is thy apparel red, and thy garments like his that treads in the wine press?" (Is 63: 2).

"I looked, but there was no one to help; I was appalled, but there was no one to uphold" (Is 63: 5).

He did not stop to think of what his disciples might afterward say: "Lord, you have gone too far; one drop of your blood would have been sufficient."

Loving Jesus: Let me never rest.

Loving Jesus: Let me never stop advancing.

Loving Jesus: Let my love never grow cold.

Loving Jesus: I want to do great things for you.

There, under the cross, let us make a determined resolution never to be, in a worldly sense, prudent. The basic problem facing people today is a serious one, and I do not think that a generation of shy, young men and women will ever find a solution for it—certainly not, at any rate, in time for the dawning of the new millennium. We might have to wait till yet another century has gone by. But . . . do you want to wait?

Do you not want to do something to infect others with a holy daring—something to change the hearts of those who now laugh at this unknown God of ours? There are other daring persons with us: Peter, who denied that he knew the Nazarene; James and John, who likewise fell asleep in the garden; and Thomas, who could be called the father of empiricists. Daring, too, are all those who were discussing on the road which of them would be first in the kingdom of heaven, and Mary Magdalene, the woman from whom Jesus "cast out seven demons" (Mk 16: 9).

See what God's grace can do? You have no need to fear. We will persist in our daring, we will ask forgiveness for the useless way we've been living our lives, and the Lord will give us new strength.

Forward! God's saints must fight tirelessly. Quickly—very quickly! We cannot be complacent or cool: we are marching with God!

FOLLY

In order to feel forever young, the Christian must cultivate, among other virtues, daring, generosity, and cheerfulness.

Daring is quite compatible with holy prudence; generosity, with common sense; cheerfulness, with objectivity. They are the opposites of cowardice, selfishness, and pessimism.

Daring is courage. To be daring is to take advantage of all available and legitimate means to forge ahead on every level, and in every aspect, of one's life, regardless of one's social status.

"The sons of this world are wiser in their own generation than the sons of light" (Lk 16: 8). We seem to have forgotten that reproach made to us by Jesus, just as we have forgotten so many other things in the gospel. This part of the Bible, so divine and so very human, is an inexhaustible treasure for anyone who approaches it with simplicity and in a spirit of prayer. Many Christians, very many, know it only through allusions and quotations. That is why they discover only what others have discovered before them. They have never bothered to stop and read it for themselves directly, without any intermediaries.

The whole world is in the hands of the daring. To be daring means to achieve today what tomorrow's generation will want. To be daring means to be half a century ahead of others. Those who think of nothing but prudence live, at best, only the innocence of doves. If we are daring, we will not forget the other half of the coin: the wisdom of the serpents. (See Mt 10: 16.) Prudence is a cardinal virtue, but so also is fortitude. If you want to be a Christian in deed and in truth, then, with all the nerve of a prophet, you must venture forth and never be silent, never let yourself be overcome by temptations to cowardice, which so often hides under the respectable-sounding name of "prudence." If you are a real Christian, a daring and enthusiastic Christian, you will certainly hear shouts like this from the world and from other Christians who are less daring, less enthusiastic: "What on earth do you think you're doing? You're crazy! Who do you think you are, anyway—some kind of prophet?" But you will pay no attention to them. With courageous daring you will keep firmly in mind that you are collaborating with Christ in the founding of a new world order, and you will, like St. Francis of Assisi, cast off your old garments. Like St. Catherine of Siena, you will become fearlessly outspoken. And with the liveliness of the earliest disciples, you will throw yourself forward and give light, heat, all-out fire, to a society which is in darkness and which is growing colder by the day. Against the boldness of the godless, which is mere imprudence, you will pit the daring of the sons and daughters of God, which is the daring of love.

When will Catholics wake up to the fact that it is no use waiting for the world to come to Christ—that it is we who must go out to the world, bringing Christ with us?

Dangerous? Of course! Every day has its cross; but every day also has its grace. Only cowards stay home and do nothing but listen to reports of what others are doing. Fearfulness, false prudence, shyness, cold feet, are only for the weaklings. For the strong, for the daring, was written the fervent cry of Psalm 27: 1–3, "The Lord is my light and my salvation; whom shall I fear? . . . Though a host encamp against me, my heart shall not fear; though war arise against me, yet I will be confident."

Christ committed what might be considered notable follies. He became a little child to play with the grown-ups and the weaklings of this world. He took the form of bread to feed hungry souls. He took upon himself the burden of our sins so that our sinful selves might be made clean. And we can repay him with little follies of our own: with little compliments now and then, with frequent gifts, with little surprises to make him happy, to make him smile.

In the gospel we meet a woman who doesn't do anything much: she simply shouts once, and her words are on record forever beside the words of our Lord (Lk 11: 27–28). Another woman reaches out to touch the hem of Jesus' cloak, and that action will be forever related with Jesus' actions (Mt 9: 20–22). Another one puts a couple of pennies in the collection basket, and earns praise from Jesus that will resound through the ages (Mk 12: 41–44). Other women present their children for him to bless them, and that blessing of children will remain eternally (Mk 10: 13–16).

A man who is curious but of small stature doesn't do very much either: he simply climbs a tree so that he can catch sight of Jesus; and his eyes are illuminated forevermore (Lk 19: 1–10). And let's don't forget that innkeeper, a poor man, perhaps, who at the beginning of St. Luke's Gospel has offered the infant Jesus a clean manger in his dirty stable—but God happens to have been seeking that very place, and all humanity will be forever grateful for the riches of that poor fellow (Lk 2: 7). Toward the end of this same Gospel, another man will lend Jesus a donkey, and eternity itself will sing about that throne of the Messiah in the streets of Jerusalem (Lk 19: 28–40). In the meantime a little boy has handed over to him five small loaves of bread, and all over the world the Gospel will tell how those few loaves, multiplied, fed over five thousand families (Jn 6: 5–11; Mt 14: 19–21). When our Lord is dying, one of the soldiers offers him a drink (vinegar!), and he gratefully accepts it; and the mercy of that soldier will teach all of us peace-lovers forever to refresh the thirsty, parched mouth of the Crucified (Mt 27: 45–50; Jn 19: 28–30). And then a thief, with one act of faith, wins heaven forever in the last moment of his life (Lk 23: 39–43).

So, you see how the sturdy hearts of his time make Jesus happy. Look at how Providence makes use of little follies—donkeys, mangers, bread, vinegar, shortness, robbers, pennies, spontaneous outbursts, even a little mud (see Jn 9: 6–7)—in order to do great things, wonderful things, which will endure forever in the kingdom of heaven. Little follies—yes, for everyone. No one is left out.

Well, what about some bigger follies? You say you're still feeling restless and rebellious? These little things aren't enough to satisfy you?

Listen, then. I have something to tell you. There is a party going on (see Mt 26: 6–13 and Mk 14: 3–9) in the house of Simon "the leper." Into the group of guests comes a woman who must be crazy. Look for a moment at her craziness. A jar made of alabaster and filled with very expensive perfume, pure nard, is broken once and for all, forever, and with that perfume she anoints Jesus' head. The house is filled with the rich fragrance of that nard. The disciples who are with Jesus—not only Judas, but all of them—are still too prudent, too sane, to be able to understand such an outburst of generosity. The extravagance of this wasteful woman—what can it possibly mean? Surely it would have been much better to sell it and give all that money to the poor! They are so irritated, they cannot stop clamoring against her. A woman's stupidity! Sentimental nonsense! To throw everything away like that! To have nothing left! The madness of this modern age! *Why* such *waste*? And Matthew tells us that all of this was said by good people, by "the disciples."

Our Lord stands up—he has just had strong perfume poured all over his head, but he has no concern for human respect, no false humility—and he says they should leave her in peace. "Let her alone; why do you trouble her? She has done a beautiful thing to me. For you always have the poor with you, and whenever you will, you can do good to them; but you will not always have me. She has done what she could; she has anointed my body beforehand for burying. And truly, I say to you, wherever the gospel is preached in the whole world, what she has done will be told in memory of her" (Mk 14: 6–9).

Now think. Hear in your heart the echo of that supreme praise, of those words with which God commended a creature who, in one outburst of unthinking love, gave him once and for all, irrevocably, everything she had.

MORE FOLLY

WE MUST HAVE A HOLY BOLDNESS, FOR GOD HELPS THE STRONG.

— St. Teresa of Avila, *The Way of Perfection*

Jesus has just been speaking to the crowd. All those people are on dry land. But dry land is no place for the Lord's friends, for those who are intimate with him, for those who are crazy about him, for those who are in love with him, for those who live by hope. Out on the sea his energetic voice is clearly heard: "Put out into the deep!" (Lk 5: 3–4).

I am not content that you should give only what the others give. Of you I ask more, much more. You are capable of rowing out to sea, into the deep, where the waters are purer, to cast your nets and do your fishing in greater depths, in cold waters.

Christ's command still urges us on. We hear him saying something like this: "I want you nearer to me. I need men and women, daring and energetic men and women, who have gained mastery over their natural appetites and desires, who can think, who can love, who can live with me. I need dedicated apostles who can remain clear of mind in spite of the great confusion which has invaded the world. I need enthusiastic young men and women who will remain constant even if whole nations crumble. I need daring prophets to speak out clearly to the rulers of my peoples. I need some strong men and women to be exemplary spouses and parents, and I need some others who will sacrifice the joys of marriage. I need mothers and fathers who will encourage their children to accept, and put their whole selves into, whatever calling I give them, no matter what sacrifices that may entail. . . . In any case, I want you to steer your boat far from the shore. I want people who will pay serious attention to me, who will contemplate who I am and what I stand for: my curing of the lepers . . ."

You, who are now my friend, I do not know whether you have heard that call which Christ gives to his own, to serious-minded Christians, to those who want to become fishers. It may be that you will choose to stay on dry land with the crowd. Well, no matter what, do not neglect to put your talents to work. Do not bury them in the sand for fear of your Lord.

Stay on dry land, if you wish, but not on the shore. Either on dry land or out on the deep—make up your mind. Look at Christ, and do not hesitate. Walking around on the shore, up to one's ankles in water, is only for those who hedge their bets, who are ready to compromise all their beliefs, who can go along with anything, who shrug their shoulders and turn away when the Church or their country calls for action.

Never forget this: The ones who stay on the shore are laughed at by those on dry land, and the sea splashes them in contempt.

If you do launch out into the deep, then set straight and firm the helm of your ship, and let your motto be rather to die than to turn back. If you give yourself to God, do it like the saints did. Let no person or thing preempt your attention and slow you down—you belong to God. If you give yourself, give yourself for eternity. Let neither the roaring waves nor the treacherous undercurrent threaten the firmness of your resolve. God is depending on you, he is leaning on you. Put all your energy into your vocation, and row against the current.

If you are gambling for sanctity, then stake your whole life on it. And if your intention is to give everything, do not keep back your youth, which in the eyes of your Father is a most precious gift. Boats and nets, dirty or torn—God will accept them, if only you give them cheerfully.

If, on the high seas, as you row along, you come across a ghost or two who groan of despair and desertion, keep on rowing, with your eyes fixed on heaven, and let the dead bury their dead. If the nights at sea are cold and dark, kiss the waters of that sea, and you will get comfort from the memory of those who have already made this journey. If the lonely evenings make you afraid, lift up your arms to heaven, and the wind will be your friend. If the thick fog of the long days at sea lessens your youthful enthusiasm, shout to the waves, and you will see all the other boats which are going in the same direction as yours.

After a while, you will learn to read the stars, and will see that in the deepest part of yourself these words are beginning to engrave themselves: "Let down your nets for a catch!" (Lk 5: 4). You will recall the excuse that rose to the lips of St. Peter: "Master, we toiled all night and took nothing!" And then, before God has time to say anything, you will likewise say with St. Peter: "But at your word I will let down the nets." You will cast your nets, and the miracle will happen. You will have to call the others to help you pull them in. And the Lord, who is there in your boat, will smile. But your very own arms will do the work. The laughter will change to tears when the nets break, and you will look at Christ. And then he will lend a hand. The word "miracle" will travel from boat to boat, wafted by the wind softly over the waves, and slowly it will reach the shore—"miracle," "miracle"—putting to shame more than ever those who did not dare.

"Put out into the deep!" Launch out into the deep waters with the help of Christ's other lovers. What are we afraid of, we men and women of little faith? Let us take to heart the lesson of this lovely tale told by the poet Rabindranath Tagore:

> I had gone a-begging from door to door in the village path, when thy golden chariot appeared in the distance like a gorgeous dream and I wondered who was this King of all kings!
>
> My hopes rose high and methought my evil days were at an end, and I stood waiting for alms to be given unasked and for wealth scattered on all sides in the dust.
>
> The chariot stopped where I stood. Thy glance fell on me and thou camest down with a smile. I felt that the luck of my life had come at last. Then of a sudden thou didst hold out thy right hand and say, "What hast thou to give to me?"
>
> Ah, what a kingly jest was it to open thy palm to a beggar to beg! I was confused and stood undecided, and then from my wallet I slowly took out the least little grain of corn and gave it to thee.
>
> But how great my surprise when at the day's end I emptied my bag on the floor to find a least little grain of gold among the poor heap. I bitterly wept and wished that I had had the heart to give thee my all. [4]

DIVINE ADVENTURES

"AND HIS NAME SHALL BE CALLED EMMANUEL" (WHICH MEANS, GOD WITH US).

— Matthew 1:23

Adventures! If you are young, you cry out for them every day; you need them.

But your good and bad moods are still too earthbound, too much at the mercy of the news you receive, the things you hear. If you foresee joyful adventures for tomorrow, you dream of them today and you are happy. If you see cloudy days ahead, you immediately get into a bad mood. The world always wants to dream, because the reality of life is so tough.

Instead of all that, I should like you to be happy with the adventures of everyday life—the real adventures, not dreams, not fantasies. I mean those adventures that are inevitable—those which, inescapably, life brings to us whether we like it or not.

The adventures that I want to talk to you about are the really challenging and difficult ones: the adventure of work, the adventure of pain, the adventure of death. For this reason I want to make sure, first of all, that you are not left alone with them. If you were, you could not go through life; these adventures would become disasters. So, I want to show you a friend who will not abandon you, and whose earthly life will help to encourage you. He has experienced, like you (in fact, more than you), tiredness, pain, and death. This is a man who for years past, for centuries past, has formed part of the great drama of humanity. He likes to call himself the Son of man.

He is the Word made into flesh like ours. He is not merely a divinity with all the appearances of being human. He is not merely a deity with all the visible signs of a human presence. He is not a theophany. This Christ of ours has a soul, a body, feelings like yours and mine. Christ's body came forth from a woman. Christ is a member of our race. If only you could understand what Jesus Christ means to each and every one of us! He is a friend—a friend who never lets us down.

Many books tell us of Christ-God. Let me now tell you something of Christ-Man, because today, more than ever before, it is necessary that those who already believe in the divinity of Christ should understand that he is also a perfect human being.

We disfigure and deform him equally either by subtracting something from his divine nature or by subtracting something from his human nature. Everything divine which Jesus has, he realizes and manifests precisely through and by means of what he has that is human. Let me write that name many times for you: Jesus Christ, Jesus Christ, Jesus Christ.

A person who lacks faith may admire his human nature, his behavior, his power, his way of relating to people, his compassionate love, . . . but will never come near to understanding the full meaning of his works. For us, for whom faith is life itself, the human works of Jesus Christ mean so much. Don't they give you a thrill?

As a human being, Jesus Christ was like us. He experienced, he lived, he loved his work, his pain, his death, as means of glorifying his Father-God and bringing life to his fellow human beings.

He experienced—he was born in—the poverty of a stable, and this poverty became sacred. "Blessed are you poor!" (Lk 6: 20).

He experienced tiredness and exhaustion, and these became divine. One day, worn out by traveling, he sat down at the mouth of a well (Jn 4: 1–6). Another day he fell asleep in a fisherman's boat—not to test the faith of his friends, who became afraid when the waves began to rise, but simply because he was exhausted from preaching and from traveling from place to place (Mt 8: 1–24). How happy we should feel when we are tired! Blessed is your work! Do not despise it—it can make a saint of you!

He experienced physical hunger and thirst, sometimes voluntarily (see Mt 4: 2), but not always. When he put out his hand to take fruit from a fig tree, he found only leaves (see Mt 21: 18–19). And when, on the cross, he sobbed, "I am thirsty," we gave him the drink of slaves (see Jn 19: 28–29).

He felt—he lived to the deepest possible degree—love for other people. "He wept at the death of Lazarus," writes Dom Marmion, "as we weep over those we cherish, so that the Jews who witnessed this sight said to one another: 'Behold how he loved him!' Christ shed tears because his heart was touched; he wept for him who was his friend; the tears sprang from the depth of his heart." [5]

He went through—he experienced—being deserted by those who called themselves his friends. He knew—he lived—Calvary, as well as Bethlehem; the garden of Gethsemane, as well as the hill of the Transfiguration . . .

His hands cured the sores and the crippledness of our hands—and they still do. His voice calmed the storms of our lakes—and it still does. His actions gave life to our dead selves—and they still do. He lived, and still lives, in the desert and in public places, in the temple, in people's houses. And when he speaks, he speaks of all kinds of people: of shepherds, tax collectors, homemakers, farmers, day laborers, judges, rulers, rich people, and beggars . . .

Look at the variety of things he talks about. He speaks of salt, of children's games, of foxes, of early retirement, of fasts and feasts, of hens and their chicks, of flowers and trees, of a mother's joy and a father's tenderness . . .

Listen to his way of speaking: with the local accent of the mountain peasants of his home district, Galilee. You remember the passage in which Peter is recognized as a follower of his Master on account of his accent: "Certainly you are also one of them, for your accent betrays you" (Mt 26: 73). Jesus spoke the dialect of his home district, with the Syro-Chaldean accent peculiar to that particular place and time.

How I love, Jesus, to hear you speak in that thoroughly human way! You made even our language divine!

Christ knew and lived pain, and pain was made divine.

But he did more than that. He also knew all of our human virtues. Everything human in him was virtue. In *everything* human, he is our model.

What would have happened if God had not become one of us? We would never have known what to do with our human nature. We would have been afraid to do anything with it. We would never have known how to behave in any of our adventures, especially not in the very difficult ones (the adventure of pain, the adventure of fatigue, the adventure of death), or even what attitude to adopt toward them. This is the tremendously *human* dimension of our gospel. Christ, so profoundly human, is for each and every one of us the model of human life. We must have no fear of being too human. Soul, body, feelings—all are, and *should* be, human.

Give us, Lord, the grace to supernaturalize all those human virtues which you put in our souls when you first gave us life. We too want to unite what you united: human tasks with a divine outlook, the lowest things on earth with heaven itself, worldly things with heavenly things, life with religion.

Our God has decided that even that grace which comes to us through the sacraments should bear indelible signs of humanity. The very first grace which a Christian gets comes by way of earthly water; and to be absolved of our deadly sins, we confess them to men, to flesh-and-blood creatures like ourselves; and the eternal God will not stay in our tabernacles unless matter (wheat) is baked in our ovens.

Thus Christ is humbled, and the things of earth are exalted! The sacraments, which come from heaven, cannot exist without matter, which comes from this world. And, conversely, human creatures cannot reach their full potential without grace, which comes from heaven. What a marvelous union!

What more can I say? Christ, ablaze with love for us all, saw the hour coming when he would have to leave this world; and, in order not to leave us alone, he invented the Sacrament of Love. That was, Lord, really a most natural thing for you to do, given the boundlessness of your love and power. You invented something that all lovers in this world have wished they could invent: a way to avoid ever having to part; a way to avoid separation. Anyone who knows the least thing about love can understand the Eucharist very easily. The Eucharist is, quite simply, the realization of the passionate desire that a mother expresses by holding a child tightly in her arms—the desire to make herself and that child one.

What more do you want me to tell you of the adventures of God, the great friend of all adventures?

This is the God that Christ is: a God who suffered hunger and thirst so that when you eat and when you drink, you will remember him. A God who became a servant so that when you feel tired after work, you can say with him that you have come "not to be served but to serve" (Mt 20:28), and then add that you will serve him with all your strength. A God who became a child so that when you enjoy yourself, you will remember to play with him. A God beaten to death, nailed to a cross, so that when you suffer, you will remember him.

Work, recreation, food, pain: that is your human life, and that is Christ!

How marvelous it is to see in you, Lord Jesus, a heart like ours. We will continue to love you as we love one another, with the only heart we have. And we will whisper to you in our prayer, in your sacramental presence, the sweet things all lovers say. I love you, Jesus. I love you with all my heart.

THE ADVENTURE OF WORK

THE LORD GOD TOOK THE MAN AND PUT HIM
IN THE GARDEN OF EDEN TO TILL IT AND KEEP IT.

— Genesis 2: 15

With Christ in the adventure of our work, with Christ in the adventure of our pain, with Christ in the adventure of our death: that is how we must proceed. And so, first of all, it can and should happen quite naturally—for we must always be natural—that we Christians will find God in the midst of our workaday world.

In painstaking work at the microscope, at the operating table, when analyzing some strange substance, when excitedly consulting reference books; in the middle of the night, at the highchair, when eagerly listening for a baby's first word, when changing diapers; when going deeply into the mysteries of life; when facing death and feeling the vague charms of the hereafter; when working with an absorbing mass of details needing to be coordinated—we Christians feel the presence of our Christ.

When we patiently go through files in search of old papers which throw light on human history; when we start off on the laborious paths of metaphysics or psychology or some other science to study in depth what it is to be human; when depression at what seems to be the futility of life hovers over us—we can always feel the presence of our Christ.

And in the raptures of artistic inspiration we feel that we are near God, and in the most acute moments of artistic exaltation we find Christ, and we who are not poets ourselves nevertheless do understand the restlessness of poets, and why their world is so often a tormented one, because behind their restlessness—in their spirit, which remains eternally open to take in more and more light—we discover a longing for some higher ideal, for a light which is the Light. And we feel the presence of that Light.

And those of us who are anonymous backroom workers, who play an essential but humble part in an industry—what about us? When we handle a hammer or a spade, when we stuff envelopes, when our hands are dirty and our feet are aching, when by necessity we work in an environment with contaminated air or insufficient light—we Christians feel the presence of Christ.

In every human activity, in the ordinary, pedestrian life of every day, in eating and drinking, in laughter and in tears, the real Christian always lives in the presence of God.

If Christ were in your place, how would he do those humdrum, ordinary things which you are doing right now?

Listen: We live in a world in which everyone is always in a hurry; no one has time for anything. It's true for you, and it's just as true for me. Well, in this situation each of us has to make a choice: either to be overwhelmed by our work or else to sanctify it. There is no middle course. The same is true of pain: it tortures some; of others it makes saints. And it is the very same pain, the same work. We all have basically the same kind of tasks (arduous) and the same amount of rest (short).

We all have within our reach the simplest way of becoming a saint: sanctification of one's ordinary life, of its every humdrum detail. If you expect that someday you will do something big and thereby become a saint, you will never be one. I can assure you of that on the authority of the gospel, thinking once more of how God's eyes lit up when he saw the generosity of that poor widow who simply threw into the collection basket the little she had—everything she had—two coins that didn't amount to a thing. Just remember what the Lord said when he saw that: "Truly I tell you, this poor widow has put in more than all of them" (Lk 21: 3).

The details, the details—that is where you will find your sanctification. All your big ideas, if they sidetrack you from the sanctification of little ordinary things, will be fatal.

You dream of a glorious future. With your imagination you create for yourself a magnificent sanctity which will blossom out tomorrow, or the next day, or whenever you decide to say, "Now I begin."

The reality is that an instantaneous conversion like that of St. Paul happens only rarely. As a rule, time is essential for everything. And during all that time, little things. Do you not see that every big thing is made up of an immense number of little things?

How am I to explain it? I ask you, once again, to think of our Savior. Our Lord was just as much God when he worked with Joseph in the workshop as he was when he died on the cross. It does not make the slightest difference what you have to do; the only thing that matters is how you do it.

It was on this very earth of ours, as I have mentioned before, that Christ was born in a pile of straw—the same kind of straw that farmers of today throw under their cattle.

It was right here, in this same world, that he worked— did not merely pretend to work, but actually worked—in a hidden way, for thirty years, with the same humble materials that we use every day. Very many have imitated Christ in his preaching, in the activities of his public life, going through villages and towns, speaking to crowds; some have even died on a cross. What about you and me trying to imitate him in his hidden life, also so fruitful? Neither you nor I perform miracles. We may have no opportunity to speak to crowds. But we can, so easily, be like the Christ who was simply "the carpenter's son" (Mt 13: 55), simply by taking care of our materials and tools, by cleaning the floor, by putting into our everyday work everything we've got, with the strictest fidelity to the duties of our state and condition in life. To flee from work is to flee from sanctity itself; it is to flee from Christ.

Be happy: use whatever means the Lord puts within your reach to bring you nearer to him.

Work can make you a saint! Sanctify your work, whatever it is, by doing it well. Be sure that you work well. What a ridiculous contradiction it would be to offer to God a half-finished task, a job done without care, without a willing spirit, without effort! A job which if offered to mere mortals would make them laugh—is that what you are going to offer to your God? Never!

That love of God which we have to put into our work demands absolutely and positively that the work itself be as close to perfect as we can make it; otherwise it is simply a bad joke, an insult to God. It is true, unfortunately, that there are some people who are so concerned with the love of God which they put into their work that they neglect the work itself. Learn first to do your job really well, and afterward you will learn how to do it in the presence of God. Put plenty of human energy and ambition into your task, and later it will be easy to rectify whatever may be amiss in your intention.

The misguided notion that intention is everything causes the work of many present-day Catholics to be a total disaster. Things directly concerned with the service of God are done badly from a professional standpoint. What we need is some brave souls who will destroy with the whip those ridiculous travesties which so often are passed off as serious work.

What we need are architects who will design houses of worship, rather than churches that look more like garages or gymnasiums.

We need publishers of religious literature who will use their skills to produce attractive, high-quality magazines which will not lower the noble prestige of Christian life.

We need painters who know what truth is, who will refuse to make plaster look like marble; who will not be deceivers in their work, and certainly not in the things of God. God is the friend of poverty, but not of falsehood.

We need sculptors who will refuse to mass-produce ugly statues for the consolation of superficial pietists.

We need composers who will refuse to write hymns which anyone with a grain of aesthetic sense would be ashamed to sing.

We need movie stars who will refuse to mock our great Christian figures and beliefs in pointless, insipid, or blasphemous films.

"I have not found your works perfect in the sight of my God," says our Lord (Rev 3: 2).

If a work is to be full of God, it is not enough for it to be a "good work." It must also be done in a thoroughly good way: intelligently, diligently, punctually. Every work that we offer to God, let us do our utmost to make it stainless. May the angels be able to smile at our work, and may God see fit to accept it. After all, it was the Lord God himself who laid down this law: "When anyone offers a sacrifice of peace offerings to the Lord, to fulfill a vow or as a freewill offering, . . . to be accepted it must be perfect; there shall be no blemish in it" (Lev 22: 21).

To show us that the Christian religion is the work of God himself, Christ chose twelve more-or-less ignorant men: the apostles. But to show us that those whose job it is to teach must acquire the necessary knowledge, he sent them the Holy Spirit in person.

Do you need more considerations to show you how you should do your human work? All right, here are a few more. People who observed the way Jesus lived on this earth "were astonished beyond measure" because, they said, "he has done all things well" (Mk 7: 37). Jesus himself said that we should never be satisfied with producing simply *some* kind of fruit; that unless it is *good* fruit, it will be good only for the fire, for a big fire (Mt 3: 10). He also said, "No one who puts his hand to the plow and looks back is fit for the kingdom of God" (Lk 9: 62). In other words, the adventure of work demands that we love it and embrace it passionately. You say that others are not doing this, and so you feel discouraged? You are working for God. You cannot allow yourself to be influenced by the miseries which surround you.

"Whatever your task, work heartily, as serving the Lord and not men, knowing that from the Lord you will receive the inheritance as your reward; you are serving the Lord Christ" (Col 3: 23). "Never flag in zeal, be aglow with the Spirit, serve the Lord" (Rom 12: 11). Has there ever been anyone who understood more about working for God and getting exhausted than St. Paul? His reason for living this way is that we have the privilege of being "slaves of God" (see Rom 6: 22).

God wants to be presented with tasks accomplished as perfectly as is humanly possible. And that demands sweat and exhaustion, make no mistake about it. But do you think any of the saints ever let that get in their way? "We do not want you to be ignorant of the affliction we experienced in Asia; for we were so utterly, unbearably crushed that we despaired of life itself" (2 Cor 1: 8). Read that to any comfort-loving weakling who tries to claim that his mediocre lifestyle is a truly Christian one!

What the world needs today is not professional apostles who spend their spare time working, but hardworking men and women—young, elderly, and middle-aged, married and single, of every social class—who *in* their work, *with* their work, and *by* that same work will carry out a truly effective Christian apostolate.

Can you now deny that sanctity is for you? Surely you see now why I cannot let you say that while you are absorbed in that career move, that financial problem, that illness, preparing for that exam, taking care of your children, you "can't be thinking about anything else." That phrase is borderline blasphemous; at the very least, it is not Christian. You will achieve sanctity precisely by means of whatever you are doing at any given moment.

Would you dare laugh at others because of the kind of work they do? Those may well be true Christians, and not in spite of their occupations. One lives both the human and the supernatural virtues—*virtue* means "strength"—with the very same energy.

A *saint* is simply a fully Christian realization of a human being. Is it an exaggeration to say that the world will believe again in saints when it sees one who is human in the fullest sense of the word?

Offer your work every day. If your love is great, offer it every hour. If you wish to live a contemplative life in the midst of the world, offer it to the Lord every instant of your life. Do what you should do; and whatever you do, do it well. Every night you will be tired, sometimes to the point of exhaustion. At those times simply remind yourself that the lazy will never know what sanctity is.

Work with energy and perseverance until, if need be, you get so tired you could scream. Thus your mode of conduct toward God and neighbor will have all the strength of the war cry of the prophets.

THE ADVENTURE OF SUFFERING

Our God, the only true God, the Christians' one God in three Persons, remains hidden. But if you seek him constantly, you will find him. When you think, when you listen and read, when you speak and write, you are near your God. And what about when you suffer?

When you suffer, it is your God who is near to you.

Look at that young woman. It is the end of the day, and she is so tired. How human and how divine it is to be tired after working hard all day. She is worn out for that reason; but she also feels another pain deep inside. Today her sincerity, which is the guiding principle of her life, has been maliciously impugned by people she thought were her friends. Today she has discovered an approach to God which, up to now, she has never known: utter desolation. People have mocked her. Her eyes saw only smiles, but behind the smiles there was slander, and there was contempt. Suffering! Suffering without tears. Desolation without a sound, too deep for tears. And there, very near her, just outside her doors, people are still carrying on their ordinary lives in the ordinary way. Nothing, nobody, stops or even slows down.

"I am suffering—why are they laughing?" She feels so alone.

"My friends, where are they?" And the echo of that word "friends" mocks her with a note of sadness, a note of betrayal. Then she remembers that somewhere else—actually, in many places all over the world—there are others who are suffering like her.

How united she feels with all of them! Suffering seems to unite! The pain dies away. There is silence, and then only a memory of those suffering hours. Then the desolation again. More supercilious smiles, more sneers. Terrible sadness of soul.

A sob: "Lord, is this how you treat people who love you?"

Illness, loss of loved ones, contradiction, persecution, all strike with the weight of iron on the weak flesh of that poor woman. She reminds herself, time and again, of what the saints said of that same blessed suffering.

You must learn to suffer if you wish to become mature. Without that contradiction you will never be fruitful. Courage consists in suffering, rather than in rushing into battle. When you want to do something really serious, do not forget the cross as a means. O fortunate misfortunes of this world! Poverty, rejection, hatred, injustice, dishonor—we can bear anything, and do anything, in him who strengthens us.

Sooner or later you will become very much aware that "God alone . . . is my rock and my salvation, my fortress" (Ps 62: 5–6); for, in times of deep suffering, all else fails. Advice sounds like mockery, and pity is a painful hammering which drives the steel nails even deeper into your hands and feet.

At this very moment, as you are reading these lines, there are thousands of people uttering savage cries against God: in prisons and in hospitals, in famine and in plenty, in war-torn areas and in countries at peace. We refuse to understand suffering, when in fact it should be the very salt of our lives.

More laments, this time from the prophet Jeremiah. With great courage he had responded to these words he had heard from God himself: "Gird up your loins; arise, and say to them everything that I command you. Do not be dismayed by them, lest I dismay you before them" (Jer 1: 17). He had trusted completely in this promise he had received from Yahweh: "Behold, I make you this day a fortified city, an iron pillar, and bronze walls, against the whole land, against the kings of Judah, its princes, its priests, and the people of the land. They will fight against you; but they shall not prevail against you, for I am with you . . . to deliver you" (Jer 1: 18–19). He had received the divine mission of warning Judah of its impending doom, and he had carried out that mission. And he, the truest friend of his compatriots, was repaid with nothing but insults, betrayal, conspiracies against him, and lashes of the whip. It is hardly surprising, then, that we should hear from Jeremiah the most bitter complaint that one of God's own could possibly utter:

> O Lord, thou hast deceived me. . . . I have become a laughingstock all the day; everyone mocks me. . . . Terror is on every side! "Denounce him! Let us denounce him!" say all my familiar friends, watching for my fall. . . . Cursed be the day on which I was born! The day when my mother bore me, let it not be blessed! Cursed be the man who brought news to my father, "A son is born to you," making him very glad. Let that man be like the cities which the Lord overthrew without pity . . . , because he did not kill me in the womb, so my mother would have been my grave. . . . Why did I come forth from the womb to see toil and sorrow, and spend my days in shame? (Jer 20: 7, 10, 14–18).

Perhaps you will tell me that you too, at some point in your life, have uttered sentiments like these. You have, I am sure, a firsthand knowledge of suffering and helplessness; you are quite familiar with pain.

Well, that is how God treats his children when he wants to make them strong!

When you suffer, keep your eyes on Christ. Then you will include in your lament what Jeremiah included in his:

> If I say, "I will not mention him, or speak anymore in his name," there is in my heart as it were a burning

fire shut up in my bones, and I am weary with holding it in, and I cannot. . . . But the Lord is with me as a dread warrior; therefore my persecutors will stumble, they will not overcome me. They will be greatly shamed, for they will not succeed. . . . Sing to the Lord; praise the Lord! For he has delivered the life of the needy from the hand of evildoers (Jer 20:9, 11, 13).

That is how the saints take their sufferings: with songs of praise and thanksgiving. Modern Christians, the kind who carry no cross, are not real Christians. That cross, that human pain of yours, can be made glorious by Christ. Suffering makes the soul either very old or very young, but always leaves its mark. It either destroys or sanctifies.

Everyone suffers—those who keep smiling, as well as those who do not. In fact, the ones who keep smiling do so precisely because they are more advanced in suffering, more united to Christ, than the ones who do not.

Love, and you will suffer much. I wish you—and you know how much I love you—pain and suffering.

Love and suffering are two bright stars that will show you the way. On your left you will leave all your loves that are petty or dirty; on your right you will leave despair.

Prayer and the cross will show you a new way, a solid foundation on which to base your life. Listen to St. Josemaría:

Whenever you see a poor, wooden cross, alone, uncared-for, worthless . . . and without a corpus, don't forget that that cross is *your* cross—the everyday hidden cross, unattractive and unconsoling—the cross that is waiting for the corpus it lacks: and that corpus must be you. [6]

153

THE ADVENTURE OF DEATH

One day I was visiting the city of the dead, and what surprised me most was a simple slab on which was carved this phrase: *Vita mutatur, non tollitur* (Life is changed, not taken away). Later I learned that that tomb held the remains of a man who was being considered for beatification.

Death is a great adventure. It is a human adventure that each of us experiences only once. But we must realize that it is not an isolated or fortuitous act having no relation with the other happenings of life. Death—be it good or bad—is a culmination of the forces which have been operating throughout one's life. One dies as one has lived.

It is human, in the best sense of the word, to feel pain at the departure of a loved one. Who has not felt that sorrow? Indeed, seldom are we as human as when, after a tearful vigil, we quietly watch the cold tears freeze forever in the lifeless eyes of our mother, or son, or best friend . . . Supreme moments of sorrow and silence. One kiss says it all. Eyes, red with tears, are raised to heaven. Life seems useless, as the eyes of the living look at the dead. Sublime moments of suffering and silence.

But that suffering, that sorrow, inspires no fear in us. Death holds no terror for us. We are friends of death, friends of that most exciting adventure of our life. For we know that just as we sometimes like to keep our joys hidden from the world, God is reserving for us a great surprise.

Poor death, we must give it back its true value. It has lost its prestige, like that blessed fraternal correction which has been forgotten for centuries. They are both strong gospel principles which we have by now lowered to the level of the rotting mess which we have made of this earth.

It is, of course, perfectly understandable that death should frighten those who hate God. The almighty Lord of heaven and earth, who for his sons and daughters is goodness itself, will certainly lift his just hand to smite those who would kill God. There is an eternity, and there is a hell. But that does not mean that you and I should fear death.

When the Lord blesses someone, very often he blesses with the cross: he is a Priest. Yes, he is also a Judge, and he does sometimes punish with a fire that is everlasting. But in such a case we are talking about the death of a would-be God-killer; of someone who was at heart a murderer; of someone who deliberately traded in the real God for a false one.

For us, for the daughters and sons of the living God, death is the great door to heaven. I do not like to say, though, that death is the beginning of life. No, the adventure of supernatural life begins here on this earth, with the sacrament of Baptism, and then it never has to end. It is an unquestionable fact: at the moment of death, life is changed, not taken away.

I well understand the terrible loss of prestige which the human virtues have undergone in this age of ours. It comes from a false interpretation put upon that teaching of the saints, "Death is the beginning of life." Now, if that were literally true, then nothing in this life would have any importance. But this life most certainly is important. Look, heaven is no more than a culmination of the forces that have governed one's life in this world.

Death is simply a change of pace: from the slow, imperfect pace of our walk with God on this earth, we will leap into the rapid and exciting pace of a perfect and everlasting dance with God in heaven. In that house to which we are going, so many who love us are waiting for us: Mary and Joseph; Michael, Gabriel, and Raphael;

Peter, Paul, and John; your grandfather, your aunt, your classmate, . . . and *Christ.*

Faith and hope are left behind us in our earthly home. They are earthly virtues. Up there, only love remains. Have I never spoken to you of the Eucharist? I think I have. That love of Christ for his brothers and sisters . . . Well, this is what death is for the Christian: it is the beginning of a Eucharist that will never end. It is the ultimate dream come true.

Christ—Jesus—will be ours forever. Forever! That is the favorite cry of the saints: "Forever!"

So, you see that death cannot be a subject left exclusively for a spiritual retreat. Death, change of pace, must be for every Christian a common subject of thought and reflection. Do not despise it, and do not fear it. It will come whenever God sends it to you. Lord, how blessed is the death which unites us irrevocably with you!

The thought of death is an incitement to speed up one's present slow pace. If it frightens you, then the sooner you settle your affairs with God, the better. You see, in order to understand death, you must be completely given over to God in life. Christians in the state of grace cannot be frightened by horror stories.

Are we to turn death too into something essentially negative?

We must not get into the habit of looking at religion as consisting of nothing but heavy, sad burdens. That is simply an injustice, and a profoundly anti-Christian one at that. With such an outlook we will never turn out apostles. How can we ever get the godless to follow Christ if we ourselves think that everything in a Christian life is subjection and sadness?

We Christians must not think up arguments to put fear into people's lives. Fear only freezes souls; by fear we enchain them. The motivating force of our actions must be love. Fear is meant only for slaves. We are free men and women, sons and daughters of the God who is Love. Love is all that will get us anywhere.

We who are free have no trouble understanding this motto which is so heavenly and so down-to-earth: "Do everything for love." Love is the real meaning—the radically positive meaning—of our life on this earth.

Poor death—we have covered it in black rags and faded flowers. I would like all Christians to be buried with this inscription on their tombstones: "Go forth! You are going to Christ, to the eternal embrace of the Most Holy Trinity. Go forth, and snatch from God's loving omnipotence the grace to bring with you all those who are still down here and who still run the risk of not finding or not being able to follow the path of Christ which you have trodden to the glorious end."

CHEERFULNESS

THOU DOST SHOW ME THE PATH OF LIFE; IN THY PRESENCE THERE IS FULLNESS OF JOY.

— Psalm 16: 11

What a wretched world! Nothing makes it smile: not the waves gently rippling over the calm sea, nor children playing, nor colorful flowers. Time has covered up the signs of war with bright rosebuds, but the world remains emotionless in the face of beauty. Any little insect, even if it comes with the most beautiful flower, irritates the world and puts it in a bad mood.

The world is now left with a weakened will and a confused brain. Do you know why? It's because the world is sad. And that is quite natural, considering all the tragedies it has seen in such a short time. It would like to smile and be happy, but everything ends so badly.

It looks at its sons and daughters and sees them hating one another. Some despise others and call them "backward," and the others respond, "You have no conscience." The powerful seek a self-serving "peace," and the weak get upset by every little thing. It's no wonder that the world has lost its sense of humor. People want to be able to laugh, to forget for a few moments their worries about food and employment, about their children, their sweethearts, and so forth, but they cannot get away from their anxiety, and the attempted laugh becomes a forced smile. Poor world, which has long since lost its ability to smile "for real."

Has the human race gone bad? Well, yes and no. We are bad, but not so bad that we should be hysterically frightened at the sight of black cypresses and black veils. We must not let ourselves get carried away by a dismal outlook on things, as if we were acquainted with humanity only by way of the nightly news. People do many good things which are never mentioned in news reports.

We hold the secret to getting people once again to feel surprise and joy, and to stop being jaded and apathetic and obtuse. This is a vital mission for us Christians. Had you never thought of this new divine value that we have? It is our duty to give back to the world our secret, and with it a cheerful smile. There are so many people in the world who are dying of an old sadness, and we must make haste to inspire them with songs of hope and good fortune. You, as an envoy of Christ, have to contribute to the general cheerfulness by filling with a Christian spirit that spontaneous impulse which cannot sustain itself unaided, which, if left to itself, will quickly end up in complete self-destruction.

The world is full of corruption, you say? All right, then, so what? We carry in our souls the secret to the only real smile, the only real laughter. We can challenge the whole world to find another cheerfulness equal to ours, and we are backed by a double hope. That is the secret: hope. Hope is, in practical terms, faith which is optimistic and cheerful.

I mentioned a double hope: it is God and his divine works. But with this hope I do not promise you an earthly paradise or castles in the air. Ours is not that noisy optimism which is always so annoying. All we have is truth—a truth which opens up vast horizons stretching way into the infinite. From that hidden source will spring the streams of your joy.

Only those who while on earth are inspired with joy at the thought of heaven are capable of arriving there. Likewise, only those whom the prospect of a great and perfect future inspires with joy are capable of creating such a future. We are realists: I bring you only realities. Wait a little and you will see the waters which began as a trickle in the rock of heaven grow bigger and bigger and become a torrential river which nothing can stop. Those waters whisper the name of God. They bring charity and poetry to make your life more joyful.

Begin every day optimistically and with enthusiasm. When you get up, think of what you can do for God with your work. It is fatal to be downhearted at the hour when your human and divine activity is only starting. There is nothing more exhausting than to begin your day lethargically. Kiss your crucifix as you jump out into the new day. That's it: jump and kiss. You begin cheerfully.

Then you must have good humor and smiles for the difficult hours when you are tired or despondent. Remember: the fulfillment of your duty can never make you sad. Christ ennobled your work. You're tired? Good. Now, at this very moment, you are the cause of God's joy.

If you do not work seriously, you will never be a saint.

Why be concerned about little aches and pains of the body if your soul is calm and happy?

Here is a true story that may give you some idea of how Christians can bring cheerfulness to people who have lived far from Christ. A young man, shortly after his conversion, wrote this sentence: "It is essential to suffer a little in order to make up for such a blind, bitter, accursed past." He had three more months to spend before he could jump from his bed of suffering into the joys of heaven. "Sometimes I get sad," he continued, "not for myself but for my parents; they know nothing of the future. But then I think of you who, like me, have been converted, who have come back to the fold after being prodigal sons; and a blazing joy, an immense peace, takes hold of my soul. Because, also like me, you suffer, you fight, you are near to God, and you know that nothing on this earth is of any use if it is not for God."

Only a few days before our friend had to leave us, he said: "Never before have I had any use for physical pain. I think I was a coward. Only now;, when it has taken on a new meaning and a purpose, am I learning to appreciate it. I want to learn to love it and desire it and be able to offer it to the Lord."

That man, having found in Christ his hope and his joy, was to die smiling, saying to his family and friends, "See you later!"

That is the secret which we want to give the world to alleviate that great sadness in which no ambition, no enthusiasm, can survive. Then people will cease to hate the cross which is their lot, and will embrace it eagerly and kiss it with a sincere love, because from the cross comes salvation of both spirit and body.

The little crosses of this world (sometimes big, and always many)—annoyances, misunderstandings, failures, loss of relatives—these all fit together into but one cross which we have to carry gracefully and with generosity. Convince yourself of our obligation to bring to the world the smile which is unknown to it because it knows of no one in whom it can trust. We will win it over through cheerfulness.

For the Christian, there are two types of cheerfulness. The first is the kind that comes simply from being in the state of grace—and that is nothing to take lightly. Outside the state of grace no one will ever have any joy other than the merely physiological: the joy of a healthy animal, the joy of good weather, the joy of the deranged who laugh when they should cry. The only smile a Christian without grace—a graceless Christian—can have is a merely temperamental one. And it is the character, not the temperament, which is so important for sanctity.

It is possible to have precisely that one type of cheerfulness of simply being in the state of grace, of merely refraining from offending God gravely. Many people have a terror of mortal sin, but venial sins pour from them like dirty water in the gutter. They have no actual friendship with God. They base their joy solidly on the knowledge that they have a Creator who is Providence, who watches over them and keeps a little place reserved for them in heaven, but their hope never soars to very great heights. Their joy is cold, almost barren, like a rich wine mixed with water. In such persons, temperament is still exercising too much influence over the body. Any slight emotional disturbance, any failure to get exactly what they want at all times, causes them to lose their composure; their Christian joy seems to go into total eclipse.

There are very many Christians who are content with that vague joy because their life in God is vague. Such people will never have any uplifting influence on others. Their joy is not rooted in their will. If they get up in a good mood, they are pleasant that day; if they wake up tired, the whole family suffers. Those Christians were not there when the secrets were being explained. They know only two kinds of joy: that physiological joy which, as we have said, is of little importance for sanctity, and that seed of supernatural joy which God placed in their souls at Baptism. They have forgotten that they themselves must cultivate that seed and make it grow.

The type of joy which we must try to live is something quite different from a dormant seed. It is a living joy: warm, burning, with a vital force, positive and marvelous. It is a joy which sanctifies us, and it is a joy which only the generous can experience. "God loves a cheerful giver" (2 Cor 9: 7).

God is not simply Providence. He is Love. He is a friend. If we are to live our Christianity to the full, optimism is of the essence. Optimism is what moves the immovable. Optimism is a dogma.

"Though the fig tree do not blossom, nor fruit be on the vines, the product of the olive fail and the fields yield no food, the flock be cut off from the fold and there be no herd in the stalls, yet I will rejoice in the Lord, I will joy in the God of my salvation" (Hab 3: 17–19).

You do not understand this way of looking at life? It seems so exaggerated that you cannot understand how anyone could recommend it? I tell you this with absolute certainty: the only reason you cannot understand it is that you lack generosity toward that God who with unshakable constancy lavishes his love on you.

"When you *really* give yourself to God," says St. Josemaría, "no difficulty will be able to shake your optimism." [7]

You must live, not simply *in* God's grace, but *by* God's grace. And *with* it you will live divine filiation and the great communion of saints and that blessed fraternal

correction which we have forgotten centuries ago—
which explains why our lives are so miserable. Live by
grace with generosity, and you will very soon come to
tell me that optimism has become part of your very flesh.
"By this all men will know that you are my disciples, if
you have love for one another" (Jn 13: 35). There is no
true love which does not bubble over with joy.

"Rejoice in the Lord always," says St. Paul (Phil 4: 4).
"Cause of our joy!" we sing in the Litany of Our Lady.
Hundreds of similar quotations can be found.

In the Old Testament we read, "I will go to the altar of
God, to God my exceeding joy" (Ps 43: 4). In the New
Testament, Jesus says: "When you fast, do not look dis-
mal" (Mt 6: 16) and "These things I have spoken to you,
that my joy may be in you, and that your joy may be full"
(Jn 15: 11). Before praising God in the Preface of the
Mass, the Church shouts with joy: "Lift up your hearts!"
And if you really took part in the Mass, instead of merely
attending it, you would shout with joy the reply: "We lift
them up to the Lord!"

Only those will be eternally happy in the next life who
have learned to be happy here on this earth, with the
happiness that comes from generosity.

Sadness and fear are the two extremes that should be
farthest from your spirit. You didn't laugh even once
yesterday? Then you wasted the day!

If you want to keep from sin, stay cheerful. Smile, so
that your soul may live. The whole world is easy prey to
the youthful smile of a Christian.

That holy sadness expressed in weeping for one's own
sins and the sins of others, that blessed sadness with
which every generous person will be familiar, will always
lead to the joy of knowing—of sensing—that one is a
son, a daughter, of God.

Men and women of hope, rejoice! Be cheerful! Work in

a good frame of mind; cultivate that virtue. The time is at hand to show the world the living principle, the fruitful secret, the powerful and very active seed which will fill with its energy and strength the centuries to come. "Rejoice always, pray constantly, give thanks in all circumstances; for this is the will of God in Christ Jesus for you" (1 Thess 5: 16–18).

GOD'S JOYS

You ask me, with a note of fear in your voice, "But what about the gospel? Isn't it true that not even once does it tell us that Christ laughed?" I give you the answer given by Karl Adam:

> Since the interests of the evangelists, as in the case of St. Paul, hung not so much on the earthly, human appearance of Jesus as on the Christ of glory, the Son of God and Redeemer, it is from the outset vain to expect from the Gospels that they will draw for us a picture of Jesus in all its details, or that there will even be an attempt to bring home to our perception his historical figure in concrete form. In the eyes of his disciples and of the first Christians, Jesus was the risen Lord, the transfigured, the heavenly Christ.[8]

Certainly we must not expect to find in Jesus' demeanor any crudeness or silliness. Christ never played the fool. But when I spoke of cheerfulness I was not referring to buffoonery. And it is true that whereas the gospel does speak of the Lord's tears, there is no record of any laughs or smiles. However, that is really quite understandable. Obviously the evangelists did not attach as much importance to his smiles as to his tears because smiles were so usual, so much the norm, with him.

If Christ in the stable did not smile like all other babies, then Christ was not human. Likewise with our

Lady: what mother does not smile at the sight of her newborn child?

The forceful personality of God-Man swayed the multitudes. Therefore, we cannot but see in that young Prophet an attractive and cheerful appearance. Otherwise the cautious mothers would not have allowed their children to go near him, and the children would not have wanted to in the first place. And don't forget that when the disciples, in a somewhat sullen and harsh tone of voice, tried to stop the children from going near him, he rebuked them. "Let the children come to me, do not hinder them," he said, "for to such belongs the kingdom of God" (Mk 10: 14). A game of smiles between God and his little ones.

Right after that (see Mk 10: 17–22), a young man came running, knelt at the feet of the Master, and asked what he must do in order to attain eternal life. As for the Ten Commandments, "All these I have observed from my youth." Then Jesus, "looking upon him, loved him and said to him, 'You lack one thing. . . .'" Those eyes, that look—can we doubt that it was appealing? The young man was surely smiling as he spoke to the Lord; but on hearing his invitation he went away sad. We hear nothing more about that young man, but that Gospel description of him is very expressive: "He went away sorrowful"— probably quite upset. Jesus' smile was not reciprocated.

You remember Jesus' entry into Jerusalem on a donkey? That was a torrent of joy. Do you think it's possible that this man who said, "Let not your hearts be troubled" (Jn 14: 1), this man who set out to "do and teach" (Acts 1: 1), went through life dejected? How could a morose man have said, "These things I speak in the world, that they may have my joy fulfilled in themselves" (Jn 17: 13)?

Again, seventy-two disciples return from the mission the Lord has entrusted to them: the announcement of the coming of the kingdom of God. They return full of exuberance, exclaiming jubilantly: "Lord, even the demons are subject to us in your name!" (Lk 10: 17). Can you imagine that scene of wild rejoicing among those six dozen disciples who have so recently discovered for themselves the power which Christ has given them? Now try to imagine Christ somber, sullen, dull. You must agree that he would hardly fit in with this otherwise bright, colorful picture. How could a gloomy man have said, "Blessed are the eyes which see what you see" (Lk 10: 23)?

At the Resurrection the apostles show a boundless joy. Do you think Christ did not share it?

Christ, our cheerful Christ, was called a glutton and a drunkard simply because he ate and drank with all kinds of people; he was called a friend of tax collectors and "sinners" because he took part in their feasts and celebrations (see Mt 11: 19). And don't forget, he performed his very first miracle at a marriage feast. Surely you don't think Christ was there with a serious face while all the others were laughing happily!

What has happened to us Christians, that we have come to look at life as nothing but a series of trials and tribulations? Is it a depressing thought to realize that a heaven awaits us with everything good and great and beautiful?

Come on, be happy! The time is here to reveal our secret to the world: the enormous joy of the sons and daughters of God.

6. IN THE WORLD

"I DO NOT PRAY THAT THOU SHOULDST TAKE THEM
OUT OF THE WORLD, BUT THAT THOU SHOULDST KEEP THEM
FROM THE EVIL ONE."

— John 17: 15

TIME FOR ACTION

We are still troubled by the jeering eyes of those godless people, and those other mocking eyes of the indifferent. They look at us, the brothers and sisters of Christ, and they ask: "Do you have a solution to the problems of the world? Just how are you going to rescue the world from the clutches of evil?"

I should like you to come with me on a quick review of our resources and methods. With ruthless sincerity let us identify everything that is out of place or superfluous on the battlefield and let us destroy or remove it before going into battle. Let us sharpen our weapons of attack— weapons of defense are of little importance today—and let us hang up forever all those old crossbows and muskets, with all the respect due to useless souvenirs. Let us leave aside all forms of exhibitionism and of fear, all ostentation and inhibition, and let us make our advance on the trenches of the world.

The Christianity of today can never forget its duty to work hard and seriously toward the salvation of the world. We must either achieve that goal or else let ourselves be wiped out! Let no one try to serve two masters. Anyone who does will get only insults and contempt from both sides.

The Church needs a total commitment from every one of her soldiers. She needs for them to live with such an energy and vitality that their very lives will be the perfect defense of the doctrine they profess. We are insisting on the same point as always: that in order to face up to death, we must live. It is the individual—not the group—that becomes a saint. Groups will always be good or bad more or less according to the character of the individuals who direct them. Christians do not seem to realize that it is for them, each one in his or her own place, to direct the course of society; not simply to rule in society (rule for the sake of ruling), but to hold the helm of society. How many Christians are aware that they hold this possibility in their hands?

Up to now, for centuries past, it has been the "bad" people (that is what they are so often called) who have been doing the work. The "good" people have contented themselves with avoiding occasions of sin—avoiding at the same time occasions of doing good, of directing the course of the world.

Lives—energetic lives, dynamic lives, passionate, rebellious against every falsehood—that is what we have to show those godless eyes that continue to watch us. But the reality of today is very different. Too often, our lives are still insipid and weak.

IN THE MIDST OF THE WORLD

Our mysticism would be rather exaggerated if we were to take literally these words of Tertullian: "Nothing matters to us in this age but to escape from it with all speed." [1] No, we must not take this literally; and we would not want to. We prefer what we hear from that ever-youthful evangelist, St. John. More consoling, more human, are these words he quotes from Jesus: "I do not pray that thou shouldst take them out of the world, but that thou shouldst keep them from the evil one."

Lord, they want me to live humility as a person in a coma lives it.

Master, they ask me to be docile, like a child who never assumes any responsibility.

Jesus, they suggest that I just close my eyes and go my own way, leaving others to their own devices.

Well, Lord, I am not blind, I am not a child, and I am not in a coma.

It is not enough for us to admire the obedience of the stars, or the humility of the helpless, or the solidity of the rocks. All of that is good, yes, but to us, lukewarm creatures that we are, it means very little. We need some stronger impetus.

Send us men and women like ourselves: individuals with distinctive characters, with strong personalities; passionate, energetic men and women who will stimulate us into action and serve as models for our conduct; persons who seek sanctity in and through the same kinds of work that we do.

Christ prayed for his own, so, let us now—you and I— pray to him for those men and women of our own day who possess those human virtues of which we have spoken. For those saints of his who are walking this earth right now, let us pray:

Lord, we too do not ask "that thou shouldst take them out of the world." We ask that you leave them here, in the midst of this world which is the work of your hands. Since you, Lord, have to go, leave your own here with us. Leave them here among us so that we may see how your faithful ones live, so that we too may learn to live your own life.

We are so weak! Leave them, and let us live with them, so that their strength can take root in us.

We are so strange; leave them, and we will learn to live with true naturalness.

We are so very mean and selfish; leave them with us, and we will give ourselves to you with real generosity.

Leave them here, and let them go to all parts of the world. In times past, many people hated you and for that reason refused to look at you. Today, their counterparts look at you and do not hate you; they are simply indifferent. You said that anyone who is not for you is against you; that it is either the one thing or the other. But in our day, people have become so apathetic that they are neither; they are only lukewarm. They have neither enough courage to fight against you nor enough love to be on your side. That is why we ask you to leave among us some men and women of your very own. Their energy and their efforts will eventually remove those cold pillars on which the world's paganism is founded, and the stones will crumble away.

Leave them here, and let them go about the world and speak of you to those who do not yet know you.

Let them take your gospel of fire to every race in the world; and in every one of those places, may it leave its indelible mark.

Leave them so that we may learn, like them, to have true peace. But if an era of "peace" would only smother us even more in a life of laziness, of mediocrity, of tepidity, of senselessness, then, Lord, send us war, keep sending us wars, so that the strings of our bows may never slacken.

Today there are very few heresies, because very few people think of you.

We need women and men of God here among us so that we can shake hands with them and look into their clear eyes. Do you not see how cold we are? Leave them here and let us be warmed by the warmth of their big hearts. And we will learn from them to be persons of good judgment, and we will learn to pray. And we will learn to suffer and to laugh and to cry. Do not take them, Lord. Leave them, and we will learn, like them, to love our earth, our own bodies and souls, our surroundings, our friends, our enemies.

Leave them with us, Lord, . . . until you want to take them. And then take them. They have no fear of death, and we will have no complaint to make. Take them! Take them to the eternal light which they themselves have merited by cooperating with you day by day, here among us; by working for love of you, by fighting and falling and fighting again, by serving you, by teaching us all to go to you.

TODAY'S DISEASE

"IF, THEN, THE LIGHT IN YOU IS DARKNESS, HOW GREAT IS THE DARKNESS!"

— Matthew 6:23

Every age has its own disease, and the present generation is no exception. This is the age of propaganda, the age of enormous colorful advertisements. In the commercial field, as you know, gigantic amounts are spent on maintaining the prestige of a trade name and keeping it in the public eye.

But it is not of that commercial publicity that I want to speak to you now. After all, those who make use of that kind of publicity know quite well what they are doing, and it does bring them in more customers.

What I am concerned about is another symptom of our present illness: religious vanity. We live in an age of ostentation, and Christianity is in fashion, at least in some countries. It seems to me that we are trying to live a Christianity of bright advertisements. Statistics, figures, numbers; buttons, posters, billboards; charity concerts, bazaars, raffles. Today's Christians certainly make a lot of noise! Drums and brass bands at inaugurations and at the laying of the first stones of buildings which will never be finished. I should much prefer to see celebrations for the last stones.

Why are we so fascinated with statistics? One reason is that we tend to forget, in the course of our development as Christians, all the good there is in the rest of the world, and we are left—because it is more comfortable—with the bad. We like to focus on data that show how good "we" are in comparison to "them." Well, no matter how accurate such statistics may be, if all we are going to do with them is look backward to get satisfaction and consolation from what has already been done, then they are useless. They should point, rather, to the way that lies ahead. We prefer to look forward. The way before us is long.

Meetings, speeches, rallies—these things are good for us Christians, and excellent for our spirit in places where we are in a minority and have to fight against an officially or unofficially established atheism or heathenism. But before making public demonstrations of faith, each of us must try to live and to show the true strength, the real life, of our faith, not as a member of a group but as an individual.

External and noisy manifestations often serve but to help to increase the vanity of the speech-makers. Sometimes they increase the growth of that empty optimism based on the number of attendees or on the percentage of members present: an optimism which lasts only a few days after the meeting. Little by little it disappears, leaving a fatal pessimism as soon as the leaders forget the cheers of the crowd and find themselves alone in their offices with any of those little annoyances which come every day. Often the atmosphere of enthusiasm and exaltation which vibrates in those who attend the rally—sometimes to hear not so much what is said but how it is said—lasts not much longer than the rally itself. Yet, to the accompaniment of a deafening noise, plaques appear with the names of those who donated some money.

Ostentation, vanity, publicity, fanfare: all externals. Lists of subscribers and donors: very impressive-looking. And a monument is reconstructed, and bricks are bought one by one, and when we give our contributions we are not in the least surprised that we should be asked our names; we feel it is only right that each stone should carry the name of its donor. Too many things are done these days to the sound of bells.

Yes, Jesus did say: "Let your light so shine before men, that they may see your good works and give glory to your Father who is in heaven" (Mt 5: 16). And certainly all these things can be a means to that good end, of glorifying the Father. (I am not speaking now of communal worship, which is, of course, necessary.[2]) But we do need to get rid of showiness in things which should be hidden. "That they may see your good works" has been modified by Christians to another phrase in which God seems to have very little place: "that they may never cease admiring your good works." Remember, it is the same evangelist who records Jesus' criticism of people who "do all their deeds to be seen by men" (Mt 23: 5).

Ostentation, publicity! All too often the Christian's left hand knows quite well what the right hand is giving, and also what everybody else's hands are giving. The message of the gospel is so clear, and yet we twist it so easily.

"Thus, when you give alms, sound no trumpet before you, as the hypocrites do in the synagogues and in the streets, that they may be praised by men. Truly, I say to you, they have their reward" (Mt 6: 2). "And when you pray, you must not be like the hypocrites" (Mt 6: 5). "And when you fast, do not look dismal, like the hypocrites" (Mt 6: 16).

Remember: hypocrisy is still hypocrisy, even when it is in fashion among "good" people, and even when it is accompanied by the sound of trumpets. Keep in mind what Isaiah says about such false devotion:

> Hear the word of the Lord, you rulers of Sodom! Give ear to the teaching of our God, you people of Gomorrah! "What to me is the multitude of your sacrifices? says the Lord; I have had enough of burnt offerings of rams and the fat of fed beasts; I do not delight in the blood of bulls, or of lambs, or of he-goats.
>
> "When you come to appear before me, who requires of you this trampling of my courts? Bring no more vain offerings; incense is an abomination to me. . . . When you spread forth your hands, I will hide my eyes from you; even though you make many prayers, I will not listen; your hands are full of blood. Wash yourselves; make yourselves clean; remove the evil of your doings from before my eyes; cease to do evil, learn to do good; seek justice, correct oppression; defend the fatherless, plead for the widow" (Is 1: 1–17).

DISCRETION

If we are to advance on the trenches of the world, that type of exhibitionism of which I have been speaking will get us nowhere. It may have some use in the rear guard. But for those who want to be paratroopers in enemy territory, the human and supernatural virtue of discretion is absolutely essential.

We want to transform this world of ours in the same way that the first Christians transformed theirs. We want to go about it quietly, without fanfare, without noise, without publicity, but with the effectiveness and efficiency of the first centuries of the Christian transformation. We have no wish to be original in the means we use. The old means are quite sufficient: the cross and the gospel.

We want to work silently. We want to be like Jesus in the thirty years of his hidden life. Everything we do—all that cheerfulness we bring to the world, all that struggle in our interior life, those ideals, that apostolate, that divine message for today's world, that war which brings with it peace—we must do all that good work silently, without any show, with a deep individual and collective humility. The proud can never understand those who try to work in a hidden way, and that is not surprising. For if you do your work in a hidden way, then neither personal vanity nor that haughty group spirit which is also pride, nor any desire of being noticed, nor affectation, nor moodiness, nor ostentation, nor recklessness will find a way into your soul, and only "your Father who sees in secret will reward you" (Mt 6: 18).

Do you not see that God, who is Perfection itself, remains hidden? Perhaps you are thinking that people will have more esteem for our work if we publicize it and let it be seen. Well, what does it matter to us what people think, or how much they esteem us? You're thinking that silence will never attract the attention of the pagans, that they will never hear of our good works and therefore will never join our ranks? Calm down for a moment. We must not expect them to come to us; it is we who have to go to them.

Because we are sons and daughters of God, we must use divine methods. Think about this passage from the gospel: "Now it happened that as he was praying alone the disciples were with him; and he asked them, 'Who do the people say that I am?' And they answered, 'John the Baptist; but others say, Elijah; and others, that one of the old prophets has risen.' And he said to them, 'But who do you say that I am?' And Peter answered, 'The Christ of God.' But he charged and commanded them to tell this to no one" (Lk 9: 18–21).

The point is, to borrow the words of St. Josemaría, precisely this: "Contempt and persecution are blessed signs of divine favor, but there is no proof and sign of favor more beautiful than this: to pass unnoticed." [3] The personality of Christ will be made manifest in his own good time.

On one occasion, Christ's friends, still doubting, urged him to take some steps of the deliberately conspicuous type that we have been discussing. "Leave here," they said, "and go to Judea, that your disciples may see the works you are doing. For no man works in secret if he seeks to be known openly. If you do these things, show yourself to the world" (Jn 7: 34). Is that not exactly what today's Christians want? But you know the answer the Lord ultimately gave. John tells us that "after his brethren had gone up to the feast, then he also went up, not publicly but in private" (Jn 7: 10). He was really interested in the world, even to the point of dying for it. But he set out for the feast not openly, not conspicuously, but "in private"; in other words, trying to keep himself hidden.

The kind of people we are now discussing are scandalized by this way of behaving—the way of Christ himself. And I, in turn, am sick and tired of having to put up with the stupidities and indiscretions of such people. They are fools. Publicity and ostentation have by now become so taken for granted that many people are incapable of understanding what discretion means. Well, let them continue with whatever procedure they think best, but may they leave in peace those others who, out of a most holy delicacy, prefer not to speak of what they are doing. "He who speaks on his own authority seeks his own glory; but he who seeks the glory of him who sent him is true, and in him there is no falsehood" (Jn 7: 18).

Discretion: a virtue practiced by a hidden God, by a silent virgin, by a Christ who escapes from the applause of the mob. If anyone claims to know the gospel and yet does not understand the value of discretion, let that person, together with the rest of us, pray to God for a little common sense.

All of you Christian mothers and daughters, fathers and sons, factory workers, office workers, artists, legislators, students, who are working quietly in the sacred light of discretion: do not be discouraged by all those "godless and silly myths" (1 Tim 4: 7). Have pity on those who do not understand you; within fifty years they will understand all too well. Live fearlessly in that liberty of which Scripture speaks. Do not allow them to impose hindrances and old-fashioned strictures which would chain you down to the inactivity so common in these times. You're afraid those people will accuse you of hypocrisy? Of a lack of forthrightness? Let me remind you once more: "hypocrites" is what the Lord called those who wore sad faces when they fasted, and those who ceremoniously called attention to their works, and those who turned the house of God into a marketplace. You will be blessed if you transform the business offices, the factories, the marketplaces, the universities, the residences, the streets, the public parks, into houses of God.

Any person who out of mere curiosity asks you, "By what authority are you doing these things, and who gave you this authority?" should be given the same response that Christ gave: "I also will ask you a question . . ." (Mt 21: 23–24). An indiscreet question should never receive an answer.

Silence is not an escape hatch for those who are afraid to speak up; it is a safeguard for those who do not want all their energy to escape through their mouths. Discretion does not, therefore, always mean silence. When the moment comes—if it comes—to say something to a person's face, go ahead and say it. In such a case "discretion" would simply be a mask for cowardice.

Holy discretion and holy forthrightness are two virtues which the world is at last beginning, little by little, to recognize as such.

The angel who leads Tobias to Rages, a city in Media, passes himself off as a man by posing as "Azarius," the son of a distant relative (see Tob 5: 12). On his return he calls aside Tobias and his father and says to them: "I will not conceal anything from you." Up to then his conduct has been the epitome of discretion, but when the hour comes for the revelation, he says straight out: "I am Raphael, one of the seven holy angels who present the prayers of the saints and enter into the presence of the glory of the Holy One" (Tob 12: 11, 15).

We must, as I have said, be very understanding of those who do not understand us. It is holy and pleasing to God for us to exercise divine discretion, to remain hidden as he remained hidden in the stable and on the cross, and as he still remains hidden in the living Host. At the same time, it is also holy and pleasing to God for us to live openly and forthrightly in divine filiation, as he did in his preaching (both to the authorities and to the multitudes) and through his works of mercy.

What we need is a fearless forthrightness, a steadfast refusal to compromise, in things of the spirit, in honor, in doctrine, combined with a refined discretion and an appreciative attitude toward all the workers in the Lord's vineyard.

The Church of Rome is a good mother who opens her

arms to all the ways chosen by her children. She blesses noise, and she blesses silence. In the Church there is room for everyone: the poor and the powerful; those of every color and nationality; those in the forefront and those behind the scenes. To all the sons and daughters of God she gives her blessing, her support, her loving embrace.

FEAR

But what about those three terrible enemies of your soul: the world, the flesh, and the devil? How should you deal with them?

Concerning the flesh, let your own experience advise you.

The devil is a real fact—and the miracle is another—at which people today smile rather indifferently. That the devil is no longer spoken of is in itself a victory of hell over the human race. As for miracles, they are as real as God himself. No, I am not saying that I expect you to work miracles. But I am saying that if we had a little more of a supernatural outlook, many extraordinary manifestations of Christ would make themselves felt in our souls.

And the world? The vast majority of men and women, all those who are indifferent to the things of God, have their eyes so blinded that they do not see the world as an enemy—which it is, and a powerful one. They do not see it in this light because they themselves are so worldly; for them, living in the world means living for its applause. Those friends of the world are terrified at the thought of death, which is precisely the severing of one's connection with the world. The strongest virtue those poor souls possess is frivolity. They live without any depth of concern, never thinking of the greatest dangers which life holds.

Another attitude, equally dangerous, is that taken by the shy and bashful. I can see the devil jumping for joy among the souls of so many people, shouting in their ears: "Flee! Escape from the world! Run away from it all! Preserve yourself from evil; keep away from those depraved souls; do not let their malice infect you!" He might just as well say: "Do not fight to conquer the world; let me conquer it." That satanic sophistry dominates the mentality of many Christians. They live under a cloud of terror. They try their best to escape from the world, because it frightens them. And as they go along their own way, they leave in the thorny brambles of the world the souls of many relatives, friends, and acquaintances.

The only part of the divine law which has taken root in those minds is the negative, thou-shalt-not part. For them it's all prohibitions, impediments, hindrances to human activity—"Thou shalt not commit adultery," "Thou shalt not steal," and so forth—and all they feel is terror, fear, suspicion. Not the salutary "fear of the Lord" that the Bible speaks of, but a fear of the difficulties involved in that. People are afraid of the world, afraid of other people, afraid of Love itself. What a terrible contradiction of the principles of Christianity! But that is the attitude being fostered among all kinds of Christians: old men and young boys, young girls and old women . . . The children grow up with one horrible certainty in their hearts—that the world holds only dangers and calamities—and a great apathetic and inert abstentionism begins to take control of their value system. In the streets, in work and in play, this advice begins to circulate among people: "People are bad; escape from the world, quickly!" Our moral code becomes but a collection of don'ts; our religion becomes a policy of abstention; our life becomes a cowardly and therefore meaningless passage through the world.

We Christians should adopt a very different attitude. We should see the world as an enemy, yes, but an enemy whose life we have to save; an enemy we have to bring to salvation. Flee from others? Never! Instead—love them!

"The commandments, 'You shall not commit adultery. You shall not kill, You shall not steal, You shall not covet,' and any other commandment, are summed up in this sentence, 'You shall love your neighbor as yourself': Love does no wrong to a neighbor; therefore love is the fulfilling of the law" (Rom 13:9). This summation has not been given the attention it deserves. It is time for us to take it to heart.

The Apostle encourages us; and so, with God, with the Church, with Peter and with Paul, we will not hesitate to shout out loud: "We are not one bit afraid of the world!"

We reckon with suffering, with failures, with the obstinacy of the flesh, with the falsehood of those around us; we reckon with all possible dangers; we reckon with our fragility. But we reckon also—and never forget this—with the strength of God. How can we be afraid of anything or anyone? How could we be afraid even if we were living among devils?

These remarks must not be interpreted as a slight on those generous souls who have been called by God to retreat from the world into a life of silence and seclusion. I bless those souls with all my heart. The Lord in a special way chooses them for himself on earth, before death brings them to the glory of heaven. They are his crown. We who are to live in the dust of the roads, as Christians called by God to work in the midst of the world, rely on those silent souls for their support.

But as for you, your field of action is the world itself. It is in the world that you will have to achieve sanctity; it is in the world that you must keep fighting until death destroys your body to make its resurrection possible. When you go into the world, have no fear: you are a child of God. Set out into each day with a steady step, and look toward the sun. Have no fear of life. We are friends of the light. We are interested in the world, and we despise nothing in it.

Love everyone.

Love the earth.

Love your body. It is the companion of your soul; why should you forget it? God, who created everything with his word, formed your human body with tender, loving care; why should you not love it?

Love your profession madly: it is a wonderful instrument which God has put at your disposal on earth to get you, and many others along with you, to heaven. For you there can be nothing on this earth that is not important. Familiarity with the world will make you more human, will form your character, will give you energy. From there you will go on to sanctify your environment.

A courageous and optimistic person, full of energy and steeped in faith, can transform the world around him with an astonishing ease. Listen once again to St. Josemaría:

> "Environment is such an influence," you've told me. And I have had to answer: No doubt. That's why you have to be formed in such a way that you can carry your own environment about with you in a natural manner, and so give your own tone to the society in which you live.
>
> And then, when you've acquired this spirit, I'm sure you'll tell me with all the amazement of the early disciples as they contemplated the first fruits of the miracles performed by their hands in Christ's name: "How great is our influence on our environment!" [+]

Why should we despise this earth? Why should we despise this world in which men and women become saints? It is here, in this world, that Christ, perfect God and perfect human being, voluntarily lived thirty-three years among us. It is here on this earth, which people so often say they despise, that the man who had the greatest personality of all time voluntarily developed that personality. There never has been or will be a personality to rival his. How, then, can we despise this life, if the hand of Christ has sanctified it?

It is here, too, on this earth, that our first sisters and brothers, the early Christians, became strong by struggling. Death scattered their bones all over this humble earth. Standing on those bones today, we want to leap up to heaven to be with those shining souls.

Peter, Andrew, James, and John, the Lord's first apostles, developed their talents among nets and boats, on the seashore and on the sea, alone with the fish, sometimes all night. They heard the noise of the waters, the cry of the animals, the murmuring of the crowds anxiously seeking God. And then in the midst of the loud babble in the streets, in the synagogue, in the fields, on the dust of the roads, they listened to the Christ of all nations and of all times.

The first ascetics, where did they live? In the midst of the world—with their own families—and they were fully dedicated to God. And the ordinary Christians, where did they live? Side by side with everybody else. They never cut themselves off from the rest of the world. "Not [avoiding] your forum," declares Tertullian, "not [avoiding] your meat-market, . . . your baths, shops, factories, your inns and market-days, and the rest of the life of buying and selling, we live with you—in this world. We sail ships, we, like you, and along with you; we go to the wars, to the country, to market with you. Our arts and yours work together; our labor is openly at your service." [5]

The anonymous *Epistle to Diognetus* describes the life of the first Christians in much the same way:

> The difference between Christians and the rest of mankind is not a matter of nationality, or language, or customs.... They pass their lives in whatever township—Greek or foreign—each man's lot has determined; and conform to ordinary local usage in their clothing, diet, and other habits. Nevertheless, the organization of their community does exhibit some features that are remarkable, and even surprising. For instance, though they are residents at home in their own countries, their behavior there is more like that of transients; they take their full part as citizens, but they also submit to anything and everything as if they were aliens... Though destiny has placed them here in the flesh, they do not live after the flesh; their days are passed on the earth, but their citizenship is above in the heavens.... To put it briefly, the relation of Christians to the world is that of a soul to the body. [6]

The catacombs of those days were not used as hiding places, as a means of escaping from the world. How can we imagine that those men and women were afraid of the wicked? The early Christians—were they shy? cowardly? timid? retiring? weak? To call them anything of the kind would be to slander them. How could they have converted an emperor and an entire empire from an underground cave? As Pope Pius XII pointed out, they did not go into hiding, and neither should we. "In the art of winning men," he tells us, "you can learn something from your adversaries. Better still: learn from the Christians of the first centuries. It was only with a constantly fresh and renewed method of penetration into the pagan world that the Church was able to increase and progress from lowly beginnings. She advanced often through indescribable sufferings and martyrdoms, and then, at times for decades of greater or less tranquility, she could breathe more freely, till after three centuries the powerful Empire was forced to admit defeat and to conclude peace with the Church." [7]

From the lips of the eternal Christ the first Christians had heard words to live by. "In the world," he had said, "you have tribulation; but be of good cheer, I have overcome the world" (Jn 16: 33). And those courageous men and women launched an all-out campaign to transform the earth into the kingdom of God.

Do you still feel afraid of the world? Listen to the prophet Jeremiah: "Hear the word which the Lord speaks to you, O house of Israel. Thus says the Lord: Learn not the way of the nations, nor be dismayed at the signs of the heavens, because the nations are dismayed at them, for the customs of the peoples are false. A tree from the forest is cut down, and worked with an axe by the hands of a craftsman. Men deck it with silver and gold; they fasten it with hammer and nails so that it cannot move. Their idols are like scarecrows in a cucumber field, and they cannot speak; they have to be carried, for they cannot walk. Be not afraid of them, for they cannot do evil, neither is it in them to do good" (Jer 10: 1–5).

You say that to plough up the world anew is something that only the strong should attempt? Well, I told you at the beginning that this book is for the restless and the rebellious. And if you have read it up to this point, then no matter how little strength you think you have, you can and should take as your motto "God and daring!"

Old-fashioned pictures show us saints approaching God with their hands raised to heaven and their feet hardly touching the earthly globe painted beneath them.

But I always think of the saint—of the full-fledged Christian—as an athlete with strong feet planted firmly on the rock of a robust interior life, and with herculean arms raising aloft a purified world and offering it to God. We must either put everything we have into rescuing this old world which is rotting in our hands or else receive a curse from God himself. "Cursed is he who does the work of the Lord with slackness" (Jer 48: 10).

SINS OF OMISSION

YOU BELIEVE THAT GOD IS ONE; YOU DO WELL. [BUT] EVEN
THE DEMONS BELIEVE—AND SHUDDER.

— James 2: 19

The heritage left to us by the mentality of the bashful, of those "goodish" people who are incapable of being deliberately bad, is the disease of omission. It is a heritage of passivity. But the great head of the Christian family sent us into the world to transform it into the kingdom of heaven—a task that requires immense activity. And he can neither deceive nor be deceived!

The early enthusiasts who followed their loving God did not defraud him. They did go out to the world, preaching with their words and with their deeds. But we Christians of today are cheating him. When do we ever exert ourselves on his behalf?

Faithfulness and passivity—you think they are compatible? Nonsense!

We so readily content ourselves with "good will." Yes, that is something, but it is not enough! Have you forgotten those straightforward words of the Holy Spirit, those words pronounced by St. John in the Book of Revelation (2: 23): "I will give to each of you as your works deserve"?

The Christian should be salt and light for the world,

for all souls. Salt to give flavor, and light to illuminate. Anyone content with a passive life, with mere avoidance of active evil, is a tasteless pinch of salt fit only for the trash can, and a deathly pale light fit only to illuminate a cemetery.

What do you *do*, every day, for Christ?

That question should not frighten you. But you may understand this one better, although it is equally evangelical and Christian: What do you *do*, every day, for other people? For those whom you might call strangers, but who are in fact your sisters and brothers?

How many barren fig trees there are, which yield only leaves and no fruit! By "leaves" I mean speeches, opinions, words, advice we give to others without heeding it ourselves . . . "I will give to each of you as your *works* deserve."

The Lord demands fruit! And that requires an active faith. A faith which is not transformed into works, a faith which makes no sacrifices for others, a faith which is not vigilant—that is the faith of those foolish virgins who will never enter the kingdom of heaven (see Mt 25: 1–13). Perfect virginity, in one sense, but perfect stupidity! They forget to take oil—a sin of omission!

"Above all, do not cease to inculcate, into the minds of all, that progress in the Christian life does not consist in the multiplicity and variety of prayers and exercises of piety, but rather in their helpfulness toward spiritual progress of the faithful and constant growth of the Church universal." [8] These are words from Pius XII, words warning us against a possible heresy of inaction, of omission, of doing nothing.

You who content yourselves with doing nothing bad, do you not hear that unhappy cry—that heartrending cry uttered by throats thirsty for truth, for joy, for health—raised straight to heaven, because on earth it finds no relief? It is at times a blasphemous cry, but one uttered sadly by the prodigal sons as a reproach to their unloving brothers. It is the poignant cry of the paralytics who have spent thirty-eight years lying in pain beside the pool of healing waters.

The Lord, the Lover of us all, will approach such people, and when he asks the unfortunate paralytics who are stretched out on the ground, "Do you want to be healed?" he will not be pleased if he keeps hearing this response: "I have no man to put me into the pool when the water is troubled, and while I am going another steps down before me" (see Jn 5: 2–7).

"Do you want to be healed?" is the question Christ continues to ask the cripples of each generation. Ever more loudly he calls out: "Do you want to be healed? There you have the waters which will wash away all your filth. I will stir them. All you have to do is obey me and jump into the water." Again and again, with a father's anxiety, he calls out: "Do you want to be healed? There you have the waters!" And a deafening roar like that of a hundred lions is heard everywhere, a roar from all those sick of soul who have left God behind.

"We have no one to help us!"

"We have no one to clean our wounds!"

"We have no one to let us down into the pool!"

Are you going to allow these people, these brothers and sisters of yours, to continue straying among the cold shadows of helplessness, you who could give them light?

Are you going to allow their limbs to stay numb forever, you who could so easily offer them a hand so that they could jump up cured?

Are you going to allow the cancer of pessimism to penetrate their souls, you who have hope—hope received from God for these particular persons?

Cursed by God be all Christians who are not concerned about the souls of their prodigal brothers, their sick sisters, their dead friends!

Are you still complacent about omissions? Trying only to avoid sins of commission? Content to pass through life without leaving a trace?

What are you *doing* for Christ? What are you *doing* for others? I would like to imprint on the flesh of your heart that painful cry, "I have no one!"

Will you flee from the world? Will you run away from all these people?

You must not commit that crime, for there are many sincere men, women, and children abandoned on the streets, in hospitals and prisons, physically strong, perhaps, but sick of soul, in the suburbs and in the slums—all because there is not a soul to approach them with an offer of help.

What are you waiting for? For them to go to a priest? Do you not see that they cannot do this? Do you not see that they are crippled and cannot move? Do you not know that they have fled from God and do not dare to utter his name? And how are they to pray when they have never been taught?

Are you going to stay at home and confine yourself to your own little group? If so, then pray, at any rate, for those women and men who do go out into today's world, who do leave everything, who do give everything, so that the dead may recover life. And if you do not want to pray for them, at least do not slander them. They belong—like you, but more enthusiastically than you—to God.

The Mother of God also lives in the world, and she loves everyone. And with the Child in her womb she goes, accompanied by Joseph, from door to door. She is in a hurry, a great hurry.

"Is there any room?" They are looking for room, anywhere. And all those people who merely try not to do anything bad would willingly allow God to be born in the gutter! This couple does not ask for money; they ask only for what someone could easily give; but there is "no place for them in the inn" (Lk 2: 7). A door is closed, then another door, and another . . . and one heart is closed, then another, and another.

So, God is born in a stable, in the company of beasts. That is the result of a series of sins of omission. And that happens every day. One heart is closed, then another . . . and thousands of millions of hearts are closed to the Eucharist. In one inn after the other, there is still no room for him.

Christ wants to work with you, in the country or in the city, amidst your books or your brushes. Do not close your inn to him.

God asks your help in the birth of his children. Mothers, never close yourself to him, the source of life. Jesus desires to be born poor and weak in the little stable that you own. Do not turn him away from your humble manger.

He is the ragged child who goes from door to door. Do not close your hands when they could be generous.

He is the father searching among the travelers for his prodigal son. He is the one who is able and willing to cure lepers . . . No matter how imperfect your own heart is, never close it to him.

CHRISTIAN LOVE

"A NEW COMMANDMENT I GIVE TO YOU, THAT YOU LOVE ONE ANOTHER; EVEN AS I HAVE LOVED YOU, THAT YOU ALSO LOVE ONE ANOTHER."

— John 13: 34

All that work which awaits us, that work to be done in the world; all that energy which we are building up in order to set the world on fire; all those virtues, those sources of human strength which we are beginning to discover, and hoping to inspire others to discover, as well; all that interior life, that familiarity with the Anointed which is increasing in us in such a way as to make it increase also in those around us—all of that will fall headlong out of place in a lifeless vacuum of inactivity if we lack love for one another. The most serious, the most deep-rooted, the saddest malady which we Christians suffer is precisely this: we have no concept of what love means. We have been suffering from that accursed ignorance for . . . how many centuries?

For a Christian, the strongest human value of all is love.

Do you want to do something on this earth which will be of use in heaven? Do you want to set out on the adventurous paths of an interior life and an apostolate? Do you want to grow in the love of God? Do you want, at least, to become a human being worthy of the name?

Love your neighbor.

Otherwise your life will be useless: an absurdity, a lie. Christ left us a commandment to be passed down to all generations: "that you love one another; even as I have loved you, that you also love one another." On the eve of his Passion, Christ presented this new commandment as the touchstone of Christianity. "By this," he said, "all men will know that you are my disciples, if you have love for one another" (Jn 13: 34–35).

That was the distinctive mark of the first Christians; they did love one another, both naturally and supernaturally. And that also must be the insignia of the new generation of Christ's soldiers. May God chastise us severely if we do not put that commandment into practice!

But, there are many people on our earth who do not even know how to love. What flame can they impart to others? How can they set hearts on fire with the love of

God when they are so cold themselves? "Look," people said of the first Christians, "how they love one another." [9] The divine and human love of those disciples penetrated the coldness of the pagan world. See how they love one another! The fulfillment of that commandment of God sparked enthusiasm. It sent a shockwave through the world. The miracle happened.

But, what can the people of today say of us? We, too, cause wonder and shock, but their cry is very different: "See how they hate one another!"

You think I shouldn't say such things? I have to; I cannot bear this shameful situation. The only solution for the deadliness which afflicts the world is love. There is simply no alternative.

Love, always vigorous and strong, as well as warm and tender, always positive—is there anything more positive than love?—has been reduced to courtesy, to mere courtesy, to not slandering, to not refusing to greet people, to not offending, to not refusing help in case of grave necessity.

Are we going to "live love" too with omissions and negations? The Pharisees, we read in the Gospel of Mark, scrupulously observe the tradition of washing cups and pots (a mere convention) and yet neglect their aging parents. In so doing, Jesus tells them unequivocally, they are "making void the word of God" (Mk 7: 13).

God gave his life for us! Therefore, says St. John, "we ought to lay down our lives for the brethren." And then he adds: "But if anyone has the world's goods and sees his brother in need, yet closes his heart against him, how does God's love abide in him?" (1 Jn 3: 1–17).

Anyone who does not love with a spirit of sacrifice does not love at all. And any Christian who hates another Christian is a murderer! (See Mt 5: 21–22.)

You should laugh with those who are happy, and not

desert the ones who are miserable. Cry with those who are crying.

Let us not be envious, for that is a sure way to end up hating one another, and then we will be fratricides.

Christian love consists not so much in being willing to give your life for another person at one given moment—which would be comparatively easy—but rather in giving to others a little of your life every day of your life. A smile, your help in their work, your comfort in their sorrow, your joy in their happiness, your sincere friendship, your thoughtfulness . . . every little thing that helps to make life more pleasant for others.

The most amazingly strong and obviously supernatural love God asks of us is love of our enemies. But we will not understand that mandate if we do not first of all live in real friendship, in an intimacy that is both natural and supernatural, with our lifelong friends.

It is said that one should have few friends, but good ones. Well, that motto, I'm here to tell you, is only for children and for adults with no backbone. It is a motto for all those who are incapable of overcoming the environment in which they live. For you, courageous Christian, determined apostle, the motto should be quite the opposite: Have many friends, and bad ones. How many "bad" people will return to Christ through the sincere friendship of one of his apostles!

FRATERNAL CORRECTION

REPROVE ONE ANOTHER, BUT PEACEABLY AND NOT IN HOT BLOOD, AS YOU ARE TOLD IN THE GOSPEL.

— *The Didaché*

There is a particularly difficult but genuine love that will teach us to love in ways virtually unknown today. This love—the giving and receiving of correction—is the great touchstone of Christian community.

"If you are left without discipline, in which all have participated, then you are illegitimate children and not sons" (Heb 12: 8). Do you know what this means? It means that not to practice fraternal correction is not to live in love.

We cannot leave the job of correction exclusively to God. "If your brother sins against you, go and tell him his fault, between you and him alone. If he listens to you, you have gained your brother" (Mt 18: 15). We must, with charity and truth, tell one another some things that will hurt. But nowadays, people do not understand that. You yourself—do you think this is an obstacle to love?

"For the moment all discipline seems painful rather than pleasant; later it yields the peaceful fruit of righteousness to those who have been trained by it" (Heb 12: 11).

Do you think it is more Christian to say nice, sweet words of praise to your friends when they are present, and then criticize them maliciously behind their backs? I cannot understand that way of thinking. Even children see that such behavior is a crime. But this is a crime which is committed all the time. Pleasant, sweet, polite words to the victim's face, and slander and treachery the minute he leaves the room.

I choose the attitude of Paul: the evangelical attitude. Before certain disciples were sent by James to Antioch, Peter used to eat with the Gentiles. But when those disciples arrived he began to be cautious, for fear of those circumcised messengers. And none of the Jews accompanying him saw anything wrong with his deceitful behavior. Even Barnabas was persuaded to make the same pretense. But when Paul—he tells us this himself—witnessed that equivocation and weakness on the part of Peter, "I opposed him to his face, because he stood condemned" (Gal 2: 11).

That is an example of fraternal correction. Such was the courage and loyalty of the first Christians. Paul never dared to say anything bad behind Peter's back. When he had a complaint to make, he made it face to face. That is the way of the courageous soul who has learned from Christ how to behave.

I should be able to trust that you, as a Christian, will never speak badly of me as a Christian and as a brother of yours. You yourself may rest assured, absolutely, that I will never defile my life by slandering you, or defaming you, or unnecessarily speaking badly of you. But everything wrong or bad of any kind that you see in me, you must tell me, so that I may correct it; telling me face to face, so that I may thank you.

"That's impossible," many people will say. But I say that the word "impossible" appears only in the vocabulary of a coward.

I am trying, not to introduce a new idea, but to revive something that was practiced twenty centuries ago, by Christ and by the early Christians. To make the world genuinely Christian, we need not invent anything. All we have to do is re-Christianize ourselves, and to do that we have to love with a love which makes itself manifest in works, a love which inspires us to tell the truth with prudence, but face to face, person to person. A love which corrects love—that is real love! That is how we will become saints.

Anyone who thinks of Christianity in a more formalistic way—more devotion than acts, more church than work, more fear than love—is wrong.

I WAS TOLD . . .

Was I told this, or did I dream it? I do not know. But now I want to tell it to you.

The waves of the sea bubbled with a thick lace of white foam. They splashed one another with little laughs, and ran together, and kissed the shore and smiled and danced away again. At evening I went to them, and they sprinkled me with their joy and told me a story:

> "Over there on the mountain," they whispered, "lives a man of God. We have seen him pray at night and exhaust himself working during the day. Go near the mountain tomorrow at noon—if you do, you will see a star shine in the sky."

That man of God, I learned later, came down every morning to the town at the foot of the mountain. He worked arduously and with ambition, never forgetting his God. When he finished his work he began the steep and difficult climb back up the mountain, leading his laden donkey. When the sun beat down on him most strongly each day, he was always alongside the cool mountain stream. His parched mouth grasped this little pain: he offered to our Lord, in thanksgiving for and union with his suffering on the cross, the sacrifice of waiting till he got home and could drink water from his well. Heaven, in gratitude, in the midst of the midday light, placed among the wisps of cloud one star. Every day.

Some months passed, and a young man came to observe the life of that poor old man. A mere boy he was, looking for adventure and wanting to imitate him. But the old man discouraged him. "Young lad," he said, "you will not be able to bear this life." But the boy insisted so much that the old man agreed to test his resolution for one day.

That night, they prayed together. Then, very early the next morning, they loaded firewood on the donkey and came down to the hard work of the morning. They both worked, the old man and the young. They finished the task, and, leading the donkey, began the climb back up the mountain.

The young man is panting, very tired; smiling, but exhausted. The loose stones make him lose his step, and he slips often. He gets up again, shifts his bag, and continues the climb.

His eyes go out toward the stream. At last he will be able to rest. He looks at the running water and then looks at the old man. "If the old man does not drink, will I?"And the old man asks himself: "Will I mortify myself, Lord? If I do not drink, this young lad will not drink!"

Indecision: mortification or charity? This time one will have to give way to the other.

And charity wins. "I will drink so that he will not be thirsty." The old man goes to the stream and drinks. The boy gasps with pleasure and swallows mouthfuls.

They both sit down and rest. The good man thinks, "Will heaven smile at me today with her star?" Rather fearfully he raises, slowly, his eyes to the clouds.

In the sky, that day, two stars shone!

UNITY

We have been speaking of many defects in our conduct which we have to correct. But I would not want you to think that up to now, nothing really good has been done. That is certainly not true. In these two thousand years Christianity has extended its influence all over the world. Pagan Rome, fierce barbarians, insidious heresies have toppled down. Even the concept of nationalism is tottering. But while everything around her falls, the Catholic Church stands firm.

Through twenty centuries, day after day, problem after problem, difficulty after difficulty, the holy Church has accomplished the most marvelous feats—even in human terms, in terms of consolidation, of fortification, of missionary activity, of extending apostolic horizons, of deepening the spirit of Christ in individuals and in the whole of humanity.

Think for a moment of the historic glory of the Catholic Church: of the remarkable magnificence of the pontificate; of the heroic deeds of those apostles who have evangelized countries all over the world; of the sublime human and supernatural actions which made saints of otherwise ordinary women and men. What other work has ever been constructed which could even begin to be compared to our Church?

It would not, I repeat, be true to say that Christianity has done nothing. But there is still so much to be done! We have to go much faster if the world is to be saved from disaster. The present age needs a united front, and there are so many things dividing us! Catholics in bordering countries cannot get along; "they" do not understand "us," they insult us, we do not wish to understand them . . . Yet anyone who is Catholic must, by definition, be universal. We should have a great love for our country, yes; but above that, a great love for the world, for all human beings.

Do not belittle Christianity by trying to monopolize souls for your own personal apostolate. We have, all of us together, a very extensive and magnificent field in which to work, and none of us has a right to monopolize any part of it for our own private work. You must have that *esprit de corps* that comes from the Spirit of the Mystical Body of Christ. No more little cliques and fringe groups that never get an objective view of the whole. Raise your eyes high, above all dividers. We cannot win souls for a little faction or coterie; we must win them for Christ.

Do you not see that individual selfishness is sapping

away the collective unity of Christians? Do you not see that the nations are rising up against their God and against his Anointed? Do you not see how zealously the godless are working to unite themselves against the Lord? How can you remain indifferent in the face of this cancer which is appearing in the Mystical Body? Do you not realize that cells thriving on selfishness will, if not transmuted, eventually destroy all unity?

National religions, racial creeds—we must get rid of these tumors. With our love we must make their proponents understand—even if it hurts us to do this because they are our own flesh and blood—that they are in effect trying to kill the risen Christ. By our own healthy lives we must bring them back to health so that the Body does not rot away.

Avoid all discussions which could harm our unity. We are universal! Spiritual envy is the most terrible of all evils which could seep in among us who have, after all, only one Lord, one faith, one baptism.

Christians, be united to Rome! Peter, the visible head of the Church, is there. Look to Rome. Pray with Rome. Apart from Rome there cannot be found the fullness of Christ.

Lord, may we all live with Rome one and the same life.

We all belong to one family, the family of God, brought together in unity by Jesus, who entrusted it to Peter, and to Peter's successors, for all time. There is no longer any division between Gentile and Jew, slave and free person, man and woman. We are all one in him.

Christians, be Roman!

SOULS

Open your eyes; look, and weep! Two thousand years of Christianity, and . . . two thousand million souls who do not yet know Christ. And how many millions more who do know him but flee from him as from a leper?

Will you be shocked if I tell you that we Catholics have too many party games whose only object is self-preservation and consolation?

Consolation. Self-preservation. Shyness. These are words empty of meaning; words which should have no place in the vocabulary of anyone.

Consolation . . . when people are killing one another. Avoiding evil . . . when hatred is in control in every place. Shyness . . . when we are being attacked.

That was not the attitude of the first Christians.

With the holy daring of that first community to be called Christian, the church at Antioch, which immediately after being founded laid plans for a universal conquest and sent out on this difficult assignment its strongest forces, Paul and Barnabas, we must in the same way go out to the world and bring to it salvation, in every sense of the word. We must shout to the world the need to slow down that frantic pace which leads only to death. We must at the top of our voices tell people to turn and march toward Life. We have to jab the indifferent and get them to do something with their useless lives; we have to get them to listen to our Lord, who has so much to say to them. Let our ambition keep advancing with its cry of "Peace! Peace!"

Remember, though, that there will be no peace until Christians win it by prayer and effort. We keep complaining about "all these evil people in the world," but what are we doing to help them change?

We cannot think in terms of worldly prudence if we wish to bring souls to salvation. We have to do whatever it takes—meet them where they are, go all out for them, never give up.

"God and daring!" is the Christian's rallying cry.

Do you desire to take an active part in solving the present great crisis of humanity? Then leave all the lamenting and complaining to those who have nothing better to do, and turn your attention to Christ's parable about the man who gave a great banquet (see Lk 14: 16–23).

As you will recall, many were invited, but as soon as everything was prepared, they all began to make excuses—a new field, five pairs of oxen, marriage—and the host of the banquet fell into a rage. You remember the rest: " 'Go out quickly to the streets and lanes of the city, and bring in the poor and maimed and blind and lame.' . . . 'Sir, what you commanded has been done, and still there is room.' . . . 'Go out to the highways and hedges, and compel people to come in, that my house may be filled.' " Take to heart that climactic statement, "*compel* people to come in." Accept, once and for all, that God simply will not allow his generosity to be made fruitless by people's stupidity.

There is grave need of daring women and men, full of grace (divine and human), who will win over with their knowledge, their conversation, their correspondence, their conduct, their work, all those who live far from God. "Then Isaiah is so bold as to say, 'I have been found by those who did not seek me; I have shown myself to those who did not ask for me' " (Rom 10: 20).

Compel people to come in! Take them by the hand and bring them in! What more divine commands do you want for your holy daring in the apostolate, in your apostolate of unlimited confidence and friendship? Now, more than ever before, we need daring and promptness in action.

Here is a call from the Holy Father, Pius XII. "All hands, then, to the plough! May God, who so much wills it, move you; may so noble an undertaking draw you; may the urgent need be a spur to you; may a wholesome and reasonable fear of the terrible future that would follow culpable indolence vanquish any shrinking from the task, and strengthen every heart." [10]

God and Peter are urging you on. Are you going to stop and listen to the advice of the indifferent who are in no hurry because they have nothing to say? Do not stop!

"Do not be afraid, but speak and do not be silent; for I am with you" (Acts 18: 9).

Continue in the same divine "follies" as before. At the corner of every road you will be met by barking dogs; pay them no heed. The wind brings you the message of Rome, and tells you to walk fast. The way is long; we must hurry.

"In your apostolic undertaking," St. Josemaría tells us, "don't fear the enemies 'outside,' however great their power." [11] And that means even if they seem to have total and unlimited power.

"Men proclaim aloud that the state is beset with us; in countryside, in villages, in islands, Christians; every sex, age, condition, yes! and rank going over to this name." [12] These words, written by Tertullian about the early Christians, should apply as well to us who have come on the scene nearly two thousand years later.

Let future centuries judge your "folly."

The same faith which inspired the apostles to go all over the world, and which inspired whole nations, in the Middle Ages, to fight for the Holy Land, can it not inspire you at least to stretch out your hand to a disconsolate companion? See how the Spirit drove those apostles into the streets and public places, into cabins and palaces, into the towns and the great centers of international commerce. The harvest was great, but the laborers to reap it were few. How quickly they worked; how enthusiastically they worked. What daring, what a magnificent "folly" those valiant people showed, who proclaimed the Credo with their blood!

Those who try to slow down our advance today—and they are called prudent!—are the people who in those days would have been public laughingstocks. Listen, rather, to the words of the prophet Jeremiah:

> Now the word of the Lord came to me, saying, "Before I formed you in the womb I knew you, and before you were born I consecrated you; I appointed you a prophet to the nations." Then I said, "Ah, Lord God! Behold, I do not know how to speak, for I am only a youth." But the Lord said to me, "Do not say, 'I am only a youth'; for to all to whom I send you you shall go, and whatever I command you you shall speak. Be not afraid of them, for I am with you to deliver you, says the Lord." Then the Lord put forth his hand and touched my mouth; and the Lord said to me, "Behold, I have put my words in your mouth. See, I have set you this day over nations and over kingdoms, to pluck up and to break down, to destroy and to overthrow, to build and to plant" (Jer 1: 4–10).

Place yourself in God's hands. Like Jeremiah, you have only to open your mouth; God's grace will do the rest. Remember, we are his instruments. Have absolute confidence in Christ. Never ignore the human means, and certainly not the supernatural means.

Daring, more daring, in your apostolate. That is what it means to have faith.

We are concerned with every soul in the whole world. You must never tire of doing good. Do you not hear the cry of Psalm 2: 8, "Ask of me, and I will make the nations your heritage, and the ends of the earth your possession"?

Never be satisfied with what you have already achieved. Never say, "That is enough." Never stop to look back. In the way which leads to God, no one can ever say "enough." That word is lethal. You must continue forging ahead, with a steady stride, setting foot on one rock and jumping to the next.

What you are out to win is heaven, and you will get there—through faith, hope, and charity—by bringing with you a thousand others.

As long as that ambition to bring prodigal humanity to salvation is lacking in us Catholics, we will continue to lead the life of mediocrity which we have been leading up to now—a passive routine of sermons, Communions, and confessions—and people will stay the same. There will be old men, old women, children, very few young adults (anywhere in the world), and no real men and women.

When will we learn that if the world does not come to us, it is we Christians who have to go to the world?

"What's the hurry?" "Take it easy." "Look before you leap." "When you're older." "Live and let live." "Look out for number one." These are the things that people say.

"Follow me." "Rise up quickly." "Let the dead bury their dead." "I have come to set the world on fire." "If only you had faith." "Go forth." "I thirst." These are the things that God says.

No Christian can ignore souls. You must go and search for souls to bring to Christ; that is the mission of every person who bears his name.

Some will leave their country and seek lands in which most people have not yet heard of our Christ.

Others will be missionaries in their own country, in their own profession.

You must despise no form of apostolate. You must never despise anyone who works as an apostle. There is room for us all in the Lord's great vineyard. The important thing is to *do something*.

There is such a thing as a false apostolic zeal. It showed itself in the original twelve apostles, on that occasion when they said, "Teacher, we saw a man casting out demons in your name, and we forbade him, because he was not following us." And the Lord's immediate reply was, "Do not forbid him; for no one who does a mighty work in my name will be able soon after to speak evil of me. For he that is not against us is for us" (Mk 9: 38–39).

Every Christian should bless the work of every other Christian. And especially if we are Catholics—that is, universal—we cannot compromise with monopolizers or exclusivists or would-be owners of souls. "Behold, all souls are mine," says the Lord (Ezek 18: 4). All souls belong to God and are therefore as free as the birds of the air.

Some organize public assistance programs for the poor? Bless them and help them. Others are more concerned with children in general than with the poor as such? Bless them and help them.

Those other people are content with giving good example? Bless them. As long as their apostolate of example is not a mere cover for cowardice, you should bless them and help them.

Bless everyone. And you, stick to your way.

If you, as a Christian, are truly in love with God, then everything you do for Christ and for souls will seem to you to be very little. And if sometimes it doesn't seem so little, what then? All that really matters is "that in every way . . . Christ is proclaimed" (Phil 1: 18).

7. AN AGE OF FIRE

"I CAME TO CAST FIRE UPON THE EARTH; AND WOULD THAT IT WERE ALREADY KINDLED!"

— Luke 12:49

FIRE AND THE SWORD

We should not be surprised at any of our present-day disasters. The world has turned its back on God and has gone in search of new gods to quench its thirst for eternity. But those ghost-gods have not responded, and will never respond, to the restless call of the earth, because they have no life.

God sent Christ to us to raise us up from the murky depths to which we had fallen, and we . . . killed him. We still continue to deny him with our actions, undermining the fruitfulness of his zeal for redemption. So, why be surprised at the terrifying things that are happening?

Do you not see a figure advancing over the earth, red-stained with blood, magnificently dressed, moving with all the grandeur of his power? It is the All-Powerful who came and who comes to save us! In a voice like thunder he says to us: "I have trodden the wine press alone, and from the peoples no one was with me; I trod them in my anger and trampled them in my wrath; their lifeblood is sprinkled upon my garments, and I have stained all my raiment. . . . I looked, but there was no one to help; I was appalled, but there was no one to uphold . . ." (Is 63: 3–5).

What else could we expect, we God-killing people? That he should not be angry? That he should turn a deaf ear to our blasphemies? That he should forget the cross on which we are still trying to enthrone him? God does send scourges to his unscrupulous people, and sometimes in the form of all-out war.

Yes, we do continue to think of war. Great armies prepare during peacetime. Earthly peace is no more than a small clot in the flowing blood of generation after generation. Destruction, killing, murders, death—the world continues on its unenlightened, monotonous course; the cannons are repolished, and new devices are invented . . . for killing people. Apocalyptic beasts hover over the precarious lives of the new, young generation, waiting to sink their claws into the steaming blood. Opposing factions use highly inflammatory language, with no regard for accuracy or fair-mindedness, to stir up hatred against each other. We are living in the restless silence of the beginnings of war. Before long, pseudo-prophets will rise up who will speak to us of God, claiming that it is on his behalf that they are taking up arms. And soldiers will march to the trenches convinced that their counterparts in the opposite trenches were born for the one purpose of dying by their own dirty, slimy hands.

War, suffering, ideologies, misunderstandings, prison camps, treachery, hunger, mourning, celebrations, "new poor," "new rich"; and then more war, more suffering . . .

We are living in one of the most difficult situations that humanity has ever had to face. The weaker branches of Christianity are breaking off, one by one, under the violent blowing of the hurricane. People are terrified by the noise of the waters, by the flash and crash of the war in the sky. Dantean clouds hover darker and darker over the pale light of the sun. Men and women trapped in the mud will sink quickly when they clutch at what they think are rocks, and these things crumble between their fingers.

The advance into a new millennium is a golden opportunity for men and women of true grit! God's justice works in its own time, and that time seems to be fast approaching when all flesh will have to pass through a crucible of fire.

FERVENT PRAYERS TO HEAVEN

Admitting their sinfulness, admitting that the present plight of the world has roots in their own lives, many have raised a prayer to heaven to placate the just anger of God.

In Christ's day the number of lepers who cried from far off asking for mercy was ten. Today, millions stuck in the mire of their unhappy, broken lives raise their eyes on high and cry out, "Have pity on us!"

As in the day of the Christ, the cripples gather beside the pool of living waters, the gushing waters of salvation. Christ, have pity on us! Enlighten the minds of those who rule us! Send peace to your people! Help the helpless! Free the enchained! Give light to the eyes of our blind relatives and friends! Give bread to the hungry! Give drink to the thirsty! Give life to our "dead" sons and daughters! Put love, put warm blood, in our Christians who are so indifferent to the tragic situation in which we are living! Shake the lazy out of their sleep! Lord, do not forget your promise to be with us all days, even to the end of the world.

Send us holy men and women who, in the midst of the world, living the same life as ourselves, will through their saintly human conduct be guides for those of us who allow ourselves to be influenced by our pagan environment instead of sanctifying it.

We need such men and women to put vigor into our millennial organizations; to reunite all Christians in the house of Peter; to teach the truth to those who have never known our God; to bring peace to the hearts of the warriors; to bring war to the hearts of the mediocre.

WITH THE STRENGTH OF THE WIND

No, you must not complain of Christianity. No, it is not out-of-date; sixty generations are not a lot in a Church which is eternal. No, Christianity is not in danger. It is young and healthy and secure. The danger is in the lives of some—of many—individual Christians. Christianity, the only power which can and will give peace to the world, was born with Christ, and for that reason will continue to grow strong like good corn until the harvest day comes. We therefore have nothing to fear: not the scowling aspect of our times, not the forces of evil, not Satan himself.

In our day—we all see it—the holy struggle of Christianity is being carried on with a renewed vigor. The Spirit breathes again with a powerful force. And what else did we expect? The Spirit has, once again, launched on the world a new hurricane which swells the sails of the barque of Peter. The Fisherman's ring blesses the young sprouts of the vine. Christians in the midst of the world, Christians who live and work there with a renewed energy, are the vanguard of the Church and an intravenous injection in the bloodstream of society.

And tomorrow, and for centuries to come, if the earth (which is still young) does not die, the Spirit will continue to send youths. When most of these come we will be dead, but we will salute them, smiling, from heaven.

So will it be till the end of time. That is how we interpret Christ's promise that against his Church "the powers of death shall not prevail" (Mt 16: 18). It is a promise that we hear with strong, firm echoes laden with serenity and peace. The force of the Spirit, of the Wind, will never weaken. And when the last days come, that same army which at the Lord's command will destroy this world will be for us—the sons and the daughters of God—the harbinger of living light, of eternal joy.

"I CAME TO CAST FIRE UPON THE EARTH."

The cries of the good who called on heaven have been heard on high. God's fire has spread victorious to all places. Even in the middle of the dirt and the blood left behind by the great war of humanity, the energy of the Christians is greatly increased. The Church sets in full motion her divine mandate, a mandate pregnant with peace. It is a message of courage for the shy, and of valor for the brave; a firm rock for today's saints. Hopes of heaven for all the valiant. All you of little faith, why did you hesitate?

Did you think that our Christ had forgotten his little brothers and sisters whom he had left here on earth?

All the crises of past times found their solution in the heights. Did he not promise that he would be with us until the end of the world? How could you doubt, all you of little faith, that the prayers of children, and the tears of their parents, would be heard by God?

" 'I am the Lord, your Holy One, the Creator of Israel, your King.' Thus says the Lord, who makes a way in the sea, a path in the mighty waters, who brings forth chariot and horse, army and warrior . . ." (Is 43: 15–17).

"Remember not the former things, nor consider the things of old. Behold, I am doing a new thing; now it springs forth, do you not perceive it?" (Is 43: 18–19).

"I will make a way in the wilderness and rivers in the desert . . . to give drink to my chosen people, the people whom I formed for myself that they might declare my praise" (Is 43: 20–21).

"Because you are precious in my eyes, and honored, and I love you, I give men in return for you, peoples in exchange for your life" (Is 43: 4).

"When you pass through the waters I will be with you; and through the rivers, they shall not overwhelm you; when you walk through fire you shall not be burned, and the flame shall not consume you. . . . I give Egypt as your ransom, Ethiopia and Seba in exchange for you" (Is 43: 2–3).

"Fear not, for I am with you" (Is 43: 5).

"I am God . . . ; there is none who can deliver from my hand; I work and who can hinder it?" (Is 43: 13).

Let the heavens sing, for the light of our God is with us!

The Lord has taken pity on his earth and has sent salvation—because he wanted to; because he is the Lord; because he still loves us greatly. Indeed, the Church has the strength of God himself, and so will never grow old.

"I am the Lord, . . . who confirms the word of his servant, and performs the counsel of his messengers," God tells us in the Scriptures (Is 44: 24, 26). And today he says to us: "You will pass like the waters between the mountains. I, the Lord, will be your Holy One; I, the maker of Israel, will be your king. I will give you one heart and one way. I will place in you a new spirit. I will tear from your breast that heart of stone and give you a new heart. I, who am Power itself, wish to be in need of you" (see Is 30: 25; Is 43: 15; Ezek 11: 19). And with a cry from his heart, and carrying a heavy cross, Christ stalks like a giant along the way which opens up before him.

"You know what hour it is, how it is full time now for you to wake from sleep" (Rom 13: 11).

"I came to cast fire upon the earth; and would that it were already kindled!" (Lk 12: 49).

I certainly have no problem understanding why the

Lord should be loved. I also have no problem understanding why he might be hated. But what I will never understand is how there can be people who are simply indifferent to the cries and the blood of God. Their attitude I neither can nor wish to understand. They are the ones whom God will vomit out of his mouth! (See Rev 3: 15–16.)

As in the days of Paul, we must preach to the nations their unknown God, because impure and envious eyes do not of their own accord recognize our Christ as being God. And to do this—have no doubt about it—requires that we go everywhere in the world.

"But there are," St. Josemaría warns us, "no roads made for you. You yourselves will make the way through the mountains, beating it out by your own footsteps." [1]

You are opening up new ways; never lose heart. Christ leaped like a giant into the middle of the world; are we Christians not going to follow him? He came to spread fire over the earth. How can we ever tire, then, of throwing into that fire pure hearts, burning sparks that will spread the fire of God to the center of the earth?

CHRISTIANS, FORWARD!

Sing and shout! The waters will pass on! (See Ps 104: 5–13.)

You do not walk alone; you walk with God! And unless you have some reason to mistrust God, why should you stop?

To preach again the unknown God, we must use the same means as those who preached him for the first time. And their weapons were these: prayer, mortification, work, a thirst for souls, the joy and optimism of sons and daughters of God, and union with the visible head of the Church: Peter, Rome.

With the first Christians we come together to besiege God and overpower him with our prayers. We know that he likes such attacks.

What other means do we have? Let us review the situation:

—A few thousand Christians who are ready for the fight. (Do not fool yourself with ideas of millions. We are speaking here of fighting; of war.)

—A few hundred more living in seclusion: a strong rear guard effectively helping the troops in the front lines.

—A few dozen saints scattered throughout the world.

"What king, going to encounter another king in war, will not sit down first and take counsel whether he is able with ten thousand to meet him who comes against him with twenty thousand?" (Lk 14: 31).

Adding up: a few thousand + a few hundred + a few dozen + certain means + . . .

But Christ does not let us finish our calculations. He comes close to us again with fire in his hand, stalking ahead, like a giant, to traverse the way which opens up before him; and we are on the march. The cry of the Maccabees has shaken our souls: we, too, know that victory in war does not come from the size of the army, that strength comes from heaven (see 1 Macc 4: 8–11).

Forward! Into battle!

"When you hear of wars and rumors of wars, do not be alarmed" (Mk 13: 7). The army of the Son of man is entering the fray. "Walk while you have the light" (Jn 12: 35).

"Like arrows in the hand of a warrior are the sons of one's youth" (Ps 127: 4).

Forward! Follow Christ! No, you cannot retreat one step. "If you walk in my statutes and observe my commandments and do them, . . . you shall chase your enemies, and they shall fall before you. . . . Five of you shall chase a hundred, and a hundred of you shall chase ten thousand; and your enemies shall fall before you. . . . And I will have regard for you and make you fruitful and multiply you, and will confirm my covenant with you. . . . I will make my abode among you, and my soul shall not abhor you. And I will walk among you, and will be your God, and you shall be my people" (Lev 26: 3, 7–9, 11–12).

Christians: into battle!

And the soldiers of God attack the world to save it. They come forth with the brilliance and energy of the stars, with swords of light, forging ahead in the cold night, thrusting brands of salvific fire into tortured souls.

Quickly! Quickly! The Church, our holy Mother, holy prudence in the flesh, is with us. We will continue to perform acts of daring. If you have to feel your way, you will go very slowly. But when God is urging you, there can be no obstacles to block the way.

"He opened the rock, and water gushed forth; it flowed through the desert like a river" (Ps 105: 41). You will see: the fountain will become a river of abundant waters.

The world is ours! Step firmly on our earth! You cannot stop! Pity the lukewarm hearts and the weak hands. Pity the cowardly souls. In the Day of Yahweh, when "fire will test what sort of work each one has done" (1 Cor 3: 13), the indifferent and the cowardly who did not take part in the battle will receive the eternal punishment of the damned.

If you see anyone falter in our lines, reach out a hand and help that person to stand firm and to walk with a quick step. Do what Isaiah prescribes: "Say to those who are of a fearful heart, 'Be strong, fear not! Behold, your God will come with vengeance, with the recompense of God. He will come and save you' " (Is 35: 4).

It is difficult to end this little book, written not with mere declarations but with jubilant shouts of optimism. I can still hear the first Christians, our sisters and brothers of twenty centuries ago, and I cannot help repeating their boast: "We are but of yesterday, and we have filled everything you have—cities, islands, forts, towns, exchanges, yes! and camps, tribes, decuries [town councils], palace, senate, forum." [2] In our day too, there are within the Church many holy men and women, in every walk of life, who are prepared to fight for what they believe in.

We are not marching toward a new version of the Middle Ages; we are marching, with Christian hope, toward a new age of fire. "I came to cast fire upon the earth." Peter and Paul lead the way. People of all races, of all colors, of all nationalities, follow in their footsteps. All Christians: a unity perfect and universal inasmuch as it is Catholic.

"The light of Israel will become a fire, and his Holy One a flame; and it will burn and devour his thorns and briers in one day" (Is 10: 17). Indifferent fools, do not try to hinder the unshakable march of God's people! They are on fire!

We are a great army prepared for war and bearing the mark of Peace on our foreheads. The world will be set aflame. We will not halt until salvation shines like a blazing torch. Our march will never slacken until the Day of Christ comes; until the bones of the dead leave the earth on Judgment Day.

"Behold, I will bring them from the north country, and gather them from the farthest parts of the earth, among them the blind and the lame . . . ; a great company, they shall return here" (Jer 31: 8).

Sing! Shout! Through the mountains the waters will pass on!

To end, I repeat the eternal cry: "For Christ or against Christ—choose!"

They—the ones who despise him—trust for their strength in worldly weapons and artillery.

We—Christians—trust in the name of the Father. We trust in the name of the Son. We trust in the name of the Holy Spirit.

And we rely on the intercession of the saints, particularly of Mary, that humble creature who, because of her total responsiveness to God, is closest to him. May the Blessed Virgin Mary teach us how to respond fully to her Son and thus become truly human, truly holy.

NOTES

Preface.

1. See p. 66.
2. Pope Pius XII, "Sports and Gymnastics" (November 8, 1952); repr. in *The Unwearied Advocate: Public Addresses of Pope Pius XII*, ed. Vincent A. Yzermans, vol. 2 (St. Cloud, Minn.: St. Cloud Bookshop, 1956), p. 248.
3. St. Thomas Aquinas, *Summa Theologiae*, I, q. 62, a. 5.
4. St. Antoninus, *Summa Theologiae Morales*, IV, 15,. 10.
5. Pope Pius XII, "Address to the First International Congress of Discalced Carmelites," in *Analecta Ordinis Carmelitarum Discalceatorum* (Rome: Curiam Generalitiam, 1926–), November 1952, p. 4. A deep consciousness of the greater receptivity of grace which is found in a person who is naturally upright, naturally noble, caused the Fathers of the Church to coin that beautiful expression which they applied not only to individuals but to entire civilizations: namely, that they had *anima naturaliter christiana* (a naturally Christian soul).
6. Reginald Garrigou-Lagrange, *The Three Ages of the Interior Life*, trans. Sister M. Timothea Doyle, O.P., vol. 1 (St. Louis: B. Herder Book Co., 1951), p. 57.
7. Martin Stanislas Gillet, O.P., *Innocence and Ignorance*, trans. J. Elliot Ross, C.S.P. (New York: The Devin-Adair Co., 1917), p. 100.
8. See *Summa Theologiae*, I-II, q. 109, a. 3.
9. See p. 68.
10. Pope Pius XII, "Address to the First International Congress of Discalced Carmelites," p. 4.
11. "Perfect God, perfect human being": Athanasian Creed, or "Quicumque."
12. Emmanuel Cardinal Suhard, *Priests among Men*, trans. Lucien Begin, Carol Jackson, and Rev. Joseph Lamontagne, S.S.S. (New York: Integrity, 1949), p. 78.

Introduction.

1. St. Josemaría Escrivà, *The Way* (Princeton, N.J.: Scepter Publishers, 1992), no. 301.

Saints in the World: Notes

Chapter 1. *Saints, Pagans, Cowards, Pietists*

1. [Father Urteaga did indeed publish such a book: *Los defectos de los santos*, fifth printing (Madrid: Rialp, S. A., 1992). —Ed.]
2. Raymond-Leopold Bruckberger, O.P., *El valor humano de lo santo* (Madrid: Rialp, 1952), p. 61.
3. St. John of the Cross, *Dark Night of the Soul*, trans. and ed. E. Allison Peers (Garden City, N.Y.: Image Books, 1959), pp. 4–45 [book 1, chap. 3].
4. Tertullian, *Apology*, trans. I. R. Glover (Cambridge, Mass.: Harvard University Press, 1958), p. 227 [chap. 50].
5. *The Way*, no. 11.
6. *The Way*, no. 1.

Chapter 2. *Human Maturity*

1. Pope Pius XII, "The Catholic in Social Life" (September 4, 1949); repr. in *The Unwearied Advocate*, vol. 1, pp. 231–232.
2. Dante, *The Divine Comedy*, trans. Henry F. Cary, Harvard Classics, vol. 20 (New York, 1963), p. 129 [canto 31 of "The Inferno"].
3. See *The Way*, no. 22.
4. Dom Columba Marmion, *Christ the Life of the Soul*, trans. a Nun of Tyburn Convent (St. Louis: B. Herder Book Co., 1925), p. 206.
5. Marmion, pp. 206–207 (note).
6. Garrigou-Lagrange, vol. 1, p. 58.
7. Garrigou-Lagrange, vol. 2, p. 83, note 18.
8. Garrigou-Lagrange, vol. 1, p. 58. See aso *Summa Theologiae*, I-II, q. 65, a. 1.
9. Garrigou-Lagrange, vol. 1, p. 59.
10. It is the teaching of the Church that through the grace of the sacrament of Baptism the virtues of faith, hope, and charity are infused in us (Council of Trent, session 6, chapter 7), and that the moral virtues of prudence, justice, fortitude, and temperance are given to us in the same way (*Catechism of the Council of Trent*, "On Baptism," no. 42).
11. See *Summa Theologiae*, I-II, q. 68, a. 2, ad 3.
12. [This book was first published in 1948, in Madrid. —Ed.]
13. Marmion, p. 227.
14. When I say "exclusively" I do not mean to negate the importance of the divine action, which, according to St. Thomas's doctrine of physical premotion (which I consider to be the basis of his system), precedes every creaturely activity.
15. Marmion, p. 229.

16. Josef Sellmair, *The Priest in the World*, trans. Brian Battershaw (Westminster, Md.: The Newman Press, 1954), p. 20.

17. St. Francis de Sales, *Practical Piety* (Baltimore, Md.: John Murphy Co., 1869), p. 17 [part 1, chap. 2].

18. Pope Pius XII, "Spiritual Lethargy" (February 10, 1952); repr. in *The Unwearied Advocate*, vol. 1, p. 236.

Chapter 3.   *The Whip*

[No notes.]

Chapter 4.   *You: A Soldier of Christ*

1. Pope Pius XII, "The Twofold Duty of All Christians" (December 25, 1948); repr. in *The Unwearied Advocate*, vol. 1, p. 92.

2. St. Teresa of Avila, *The Life of Teresa of Jesus*, trans. and ed. E. Allison Peers (Garden City, N.Y.: Image Books, 1960), pp. 137–138 [chap. 13].

3. *The Life of Teresa of Jesus*, p. 138 [chap. 13].

4. *The Way*, no. 121.

5. *The Way*, no. 132.

6. *The Way*, no. 719.

7. *The Way*, no. 519.

8. *The Way*, no. 932.

9. Friedrich Nietzsche, *The Will to Power*, trans. and ed. Walter Kaufmann (New York: Random House, 1967), p. 481 [no. 910].

10. *The Way*, no. 990.

11. St. Teresa of Avila, *The Way of Perfection*, trans. and ed. E. Allison Peers (Garden City, N.Y.: Image Books, 1964), p. 150 [chap. 21].

Chapter 5.   *Into the Deep*

1. Giovanni Papini, *The Letters of Pope Celestine VI to All Mankind*, trans. Loretta Murnane (New York: F. P. Dutton and Co., 1948), p. 202.

2. St. Francis de Sales, *Practical Piety*, pp. 57–58 [part 1, chap. 23].

3. St. John of the Cross, *Living Flame of Love*, trans. and ed. E. Allison Peers (Garden City, N.Y.: Image Books, 1962), pp. 121–122 [stanza 3, no. 53].

4. Rabindranath Tagore, *Gitanjali* (London: Macmillan, 1915), pp. 42–43 [no. 50].

5. Dom Columba Marmion, *Christ the Life of the Soul*, trans. a Nun of Tyburn Convent (St. Louis: B. Herder Book Co., 1925), p. 50.

6. *The Way*, no. 178.

7. *The Way*, no. 476.

8. Karl Adam, *The Son of God*, trans. Philip Hereford (New York: Sheed & Ward, 1940), p. 88.

Chapter 6. *In the World*

1. Tertullian, *Apology*, trans. I. R. Glover (Cambridge, Mass.: Harvard University Press, 1958), p. 189 [no. 41].

2. I wish to make my meaning quite clear and to avoid misinterpretations. I am in no way opposed to collective demonstrations of our faith, to public and social demonstrations of our beliefs. Obviously, they are not only licit but absolutely necessary. But let them be only that: manifestations of *faith*; exterior demonstrations of something that really lives in the souls of those who make them. They should not be periodic and gregarious meetings of mobs, of actually spiritless individuals who become enthusiastic for a moment and then fall back into the sickly tepidity that is their normal state. How often (and how unfortunate this is) our Catholics are content with mere numerical strength, when they should be much more interested in interior strength.

3. *The Way*, no. 959.

4. *The Way*, no. 376.

5. Tertullian, p. 191 [no. 42].

6. *The Epistle to Diognetus*, in *Early Christian Writings*, trans. Maxwell Staniforth, ed. Robert Baldick and Betty Radice (Baltimore, Md.: Penguin Books, 1975), pp. 176–177 [nos. 5 and 6].

7. Pope Pius XII, "Now Is the Time for Action" (September 7, 1947); repr. in *The Unwearied Advocate*, vol. 2, p. 9.

8. Pope Pius XII, *Mediator Dei*; repr. in *The Papal Encyclicals 1939–1958*, ed. Claudia Carlen, I.H.M. (Raleigh, N.C.: 1981), vol. 4, p. 148 [no. 185].

9. Tertullian, p. 177 [no. 39].

10. Pope Pius XII, "Spiritual Lethargy," in *The Unwearied Advocate*, vol. 1, p. 239.

11. *The Way*, no. 955.

12. Tertullian, p. 5 [no. 42].

Chapter 7. *An Age of Fire*

1. *The Way*, no. 928.

2. Tertullian, *Apology*, trans. I. R. Glover (Cambridge, Mass.: Harvard University Press, 1958), p. 169 [no. 37].

P-116+